D1220474

New Growth

How My Hair Saved My Life

Margaret A. Brunson

WestBow
PRESS

A DIVISION OF THOMAS NELSON

Copyright © 2012 Margaret A. Brunson

All rights reserved. No part of this book may be used or reproduced by any means,
graphic, electronic, or mechanical, including photocopying, recording, taping or by any
information storage retrieval system without the written permission of the publisher
except in the case of brief quotations embodied in critical articles and reviews.

WestBow Press books may be ordered through booksellers or by contacting:

WestBow Press
A Division of Thomas Nelson
1663 Liberty Drive
Bloomington, IN 47403
www.westbowpress.com
1-(866) 928-1240

Because of the dynamic nature of the Internet, any web addresses or links contained in
this book may have changed since publication and may no longer be valid. The views
expressed in this work are solely those of the author and do not necessarily reflect the
views of the publisher, and the publisher hereby disclaims any responsibility for them.

Photos by Stan Chambers Jr. Photography –
www.stanchambersjr.com

ISBN: 978-1-4497-3460-2 (sc)
ISBN: 978-1-4497-3461-9 (hc)
ISBN: 978-1-4497-3459-6 (e)

Library of Congress Control Number: 2011963014

Printed in the United States of America

WestBow Press rev. date: 3/6/2012

Dedication

This book is dedicated to freedom.
Live for Him. Be free.

"So if the Son sets you free, you are truly free."
—John 8:36 (New Living Translation)

To: The Powells!   6·24·13

Continue to embrace New
Growth with grace, love
& peace!

Blessings!
Margaret

Acknowledgements

I am thankful for being able to live in freedom. I am so grateful to God for sending His *only* Son so that I won't have to suffer. So I won't have to fear what people will say once they read this. So I won't fear man and their strange expressions because they don't agree with my views. He died so that I might live and be *free*! God, through Jesus Christ, is the most important person in my life, and I love Him. He gave me talents, abilities, favor, and by His Spirit I have the power to walk toward that vision. I appreciate all He has allowed me to do, be, speak, and write. Without Him, I am nothing. And without Him, nothing is possible. But with Him, anything is possible.

I'd like to acknowledge my parents, Dr. Jesse and Mrs. Doris Brunson. God sent me to a set of parents who have provided for me, protected me, loved me unconditionally, forgiven me, guided me, and showed me who God is. Mom, Dad, I want to acknowledge that you started a legacy of greatness and love. I have always wanted to please you because I desire to make you proud. I hope you are proud.

To my brother, Wayne: Thanks for never telling me that I was ugly. You never put me down, and you have always been there to encourage me. I believe that you are the best brother that any sister could have. Marvella, my sister-in-law (love), you have inspired me through your confident being, and I know that God has great work for you. You are going to work miracles in the lives of many young women. They will love themselves more because of you.

To Zari, my beautiful little niece: This book is for you and all the little girls like you who will one day become your friends and shopping buddies. I want each of you to read this book and understand how beautiful and special you are. I want you to share it with your friends so they also will know how wonderful they are and how much they should love themselves.

To every girl who will ever deal with low self-esteem: I wrote this for you. I was afraid, but I stepped out into uncomfortable territory so that I could grow, change, and share my story with you. I had thoughts like, "What will people think?" and "People might laugh at me," which sometimes cause us not to take the risk of being uniquely different and set apart. But when you become bold and realize that there will *never* come a day when we'll be able to totally please people, we'll realize that the only thing that matters is how God sees us. And when we begin to see ourselves the way He does, there is freedom.

To the special friends who've supported me along the way: Many of you helped to restore my heart with your humility, love, and respect. You are special people with special hearts. God loves each one of you and longs for you more than you will ever know. God has given you a purpose and a future. He definitely has need of you. I know and believe that you will do great things for God and others, and I just hope to be there to witness it all. I continue on this journey by acknowledging you and realizing that you played a huge part in this story. I hope that as God gives us life and strength, you will always know the place in my heart that you hold. God bless each of you!

Table of Contents

Acknowledgements   vii

Purpose   xiii

Lifesaver One: Hair Grows from the Roots; So Do We   1
   Nappy Roots   1
   Chosen from the Root   5
   There's Purpose in the Roots   7

Lifesaver Two: Growth Is an Intentional Process   13
   Decisions Should Be Intentional   14
   The Decision to Pretend   18
   Decisions Serve a Purpose—Even the "Long" Ones   20
   Decisions Change Your Life: For Better and for Worse   21

Lifesaver Three: In Order to Grow, Change Is Not Optional   27
   Transition—Breakage—Change   28
   God Was in My Hair   33
   Accept Change; Move Forward   36

How My Hair Saved My Life   45
   I Am Free!   46
   I Am Who I Am and I Am Beautiful!   49
   I Am Strong   52
   I Am Bold and Courageous   55
   I Am Capable of Making the Best Decisions for My Life   57
   So What Does This Mean for You?   59
   Activate the Power   60

Excerpts from the Blog   65

About the Author   107

Purpose

Let me start by saying, this is neither a "rags to riches" story nor is it a story about an addiction to drugs, incidents of physical abuse, or victimization after a terrible crime. However, this is my story. It is a story that is probably very familiar to many women and young women in this country. My story is familiar because it is one of a search of one's self. So, this book is not a guide to natural hair care, nor is it a step-by-step manual on how to create some style for your hair. Rather, it is about how a woman's hair can become a journey within a journey. It is about how hair can change a woman's life and how it saved mine. It might sound silly or extreme, but as you read, you will understand why I've chosen to say that "my hair saved my life."

So, the question in your mind is probably, "How will I relate to your story and this book?"

There were parts of this book that I wrote while tears streamed from my eyes. Because, in order to tell this story, I had to get in tune with *me*. I had to tune into who I am, experiences that brought me to this very place in my life, and all the extra "stuff" in between. Through this "relationship" with my hair, I began to reflect on my life's journey. I became inspired to complete this book because of *you*! I knew that once you picked it up, you would connect with the experiences of my hair journey. This book is about all those times when you got upset because your hair didn't turn out quite the way you wanted it to. It's about those times when you decided to change your hairstyle because of something you were experiencing in your life. And that time when you just wanted people to like you for you and not what you looked like. That (plus much more) is what this book is about. It's about *you*!

The purpose of this book is to encourage you to focus on a higher and deeper level of purpose about who you are and what God desires for your life. The purpose of this book is to let you know that you *are* good enough and *you* are not *what* you do. The things that have happened in your life are due to events, actions, and choices that each played a part in your journey. You can look at those events, actions, and choices as a hindrance and distraction, or you can choose to use them to propel you forward. People are waiting on you. People who you know are going through situations in their lives that you might be able to help them with. After reading this book, my hope is that you will find support and a common understanding of who you are and not be afraid to step out and do what you desire.

My decision was to transition back into my natural hair and back to me. And as I decided to make this physical change from my relaxed hair to my natural hair, I had to go through some changes. I began to understand that this journey was part of a preparation process—preparation for a greater purpose, which is sometimes *very* uncomfortable and requires patience. I had to start paying attention to my hair and spending more time on my hair to come up with styles that looked good.

In this same way, as we prepare to reach our destiny in life, it will require more effort, greater observation as to what's going on in and around our lives, and more time spent on actually working to improve our current state. I realized that I'd get some odd stares, some negative comments from some of the people in my life, and face some ridicule. I encountered women who said to me, "Oh, why would you want to do that—you have such beautiful hair?" or "I like your hair straight better; it fits you better."

But I did not worry about *people* and what they thought. I believed that my mission would be accomplished. I believed that through this intimate hair walk I would experience a new thing—*freedom* and *confidence* in self—and that old things would pass away and *all* things would become new. I believed that this journey would bring women closer to their own purpose through this unexplainable divine connection we have with our hair!

I believed that I would gain spiritual and emotional strength as I walked out this hair journey.

I was and am willing to place the world's view of my "beauty" on the line to fulfill the *greatness* that God wants to do through me. It takes boldness and courage, but it's worth it.

DISCLAIMER: I do not have all the answers. I am not claiming to be able to give you any secret steps to happiness or greater satisfaction in your life. On the contrary, I'm sharing my story with you in hopes that you will gain some insight into your own spiritual journey and acknowledge the power within to change your life.

Also, I must state that I am not, in any way, shining a negative light on hair relaxers, weaves, or anything that's not "natural," or on the women who do not wear their hair natural. We each have our own reasons for wearing our hair in certain styles. However, again, I am sharing my story with you in hopes that you will examine why you have made certain choices about your appearance and that it will allow you to search within yourself to be okay with those decisions. I want all women to read this book and connect with the message—not just my hair. I want women to understand that I am using my hair as a reference point to discuss something deeper that has happened in my life. The message is about your inner being and spirit, and not only about hair.

GUARANTEE: If you read this book with an open heart and a willingness to reflect on your life's journey and examine your current place, you will have more insight into yourself than you did prior to reading it.

HOPE: I hope this book will cause you to rethink the way you love yourself and live as yourself.

INSTRUCTIONS:

1. Open your heart and mind.

2. Be open to the new growth that will occur once you complete this book.

3. Look for the "real you." The "real you" will begin to emanate from each page and will beckon you to meet her.

Lifesaver One:
Hair Grows from the Roots; So Do We

Nappy Roots

I cried every day! That's how I would sum up my elementary school days. Of course that's an exaggeration, but I'm sure it might seem accurate to my parents and brother. Sure, I had friends and definitely some happy memories of my time in elementary school; however, I remember crying a lot! The tears were usually because someone in my class or school called me "ugly," "four eyes," or "Medusa." Tears also streamed down my face whenever my mom would have to comb and/or straighten my "nappy roots" with the hot comb. I was so disgusted with myself. I remember calling myself ugly because I wore these hideous thick glasses with plastic frames, and I never really liked my hair.

In my opinion, those mean kids at school were right, and it was hurtful. It hurt that they saw the same things that I saw when I looked at myself in the mirror. For some reason, I'd hoped that what I saw was inaccurate and that others thought I looked different than I did. Not to mention that I grew up in the '80s and '90s, which was a time when the "pretty girls" were light skinned with long hair. So many girls who didn't look like that didn't get much attention paid to their physical appearance. I definitely didn't fit the description of a "pretty girl" back in those days.

Even then, I understood the relationship between hair, physical appearance, and my level of self-esteem. In order for me to feel good about myself, I needed to look good. It was that simple to me. And since I was never satisfied with how I looked, I never felt good about myself. At that time, I didn't want to wear my hair in braids because I was teased, and other girls didn't wear their hair that way. If they did wear it braided, they wore extension braids with synthetic hair (which I thought was absolutely great). But no, my mom would braid my own hair into small box braids. My hair was thick, long, black, and natural. What was she thinking?

Back then, it wasn't as popular to wear your hair that way unless it was with hair extensions braided with your hair. I always wanted to wear my hair "loose," as I called it then. Not to mention that after I hit puberty I started having severe problems with acne, so because my face was always broken out, I at least wanted my hair to be okay. But now as I think about it, my ideals of beauty were actually loosely shaped by the standard of black beauty at the time: light skinned with long, straight hair. So that was what I wanted to look like.

Then, there was change! It was fall of 1990, the beginning of my fifth-grade year. I was ten years old, with long, thick, natural hair, which was in the usual style of the tiny box braids. This would be my last year wearing my hair "nappy." My mom had always styled my hair in braids, and when she or I wanted it straight, she would straighten it with the hot comb on the stove. My hair would sizzle, and the blue hair grease would get on my neck and burn from the heat of the comb. I remember my dad coming into the kitchen jokingly asking if we were straightening or burning my hair. So there I was in my last year before middle school, and I felt like I needed to redefine my image. I was tired of that greasy straight hair that would get "nappy" again once it got wet. So I informed my mom that I needed (okay, wanted) a relaxer (we used to call it a perm).

And of course, my explanation was very well thought out and logical: all of my other friends had started wearing their hair "loose" and relaxed around the fourth grade, and I wanted to look like everyone else. I didn't want to stand out anymore. I wanted to be cute and popular too. I wanted my hair to be long and straight and stay that way, so that I'd finally be and feel pretty. This relaxer would mean the end of all my problems! No more being teased about my braids making me look like

Medusa. No more feeling different from everyone else. No more feeling left out because all my friends' hair was straight and I was still wearing "kiddie" braids. This relaxer meant that life for me was about to change. I was going to middle school and growing up.

So, right before I took my sixth-grade pictures, I begged my mom to put a relaxer in my hair, and against her own personal feelings about it, she did it. She blow-dried it, curled it with the curling iron, and then rolled it so I'd still have the curls for my pictures. When I woke up the next morning, I felt brand-new. I was so excited about my new hairdo. When it was time to style my hair, I told my mom I could style it. I took out the rollers, brushed some of my hair up and put a ponytail holder around it, and brushed the bottom part down. I walked into the school with a brand-new attitude. I was so happy. *I was sure that this would be the first day of a better life for me.*

I spotted some of my friends, and of course they told me that they liked my hair and that my hair looked nice. I went throughout the day all business as usual, but I began to notice that none of the people who I really wanted to notice my hair (like the cute boys and the popular girls) said a word. It was as if they didn't even notice the change. To them, I was still "Margaret with the big glasses" who they teased in elementary school. To my friends, I was just the same Margaret but now with straight hair. Nothing had changed. I felt awful. I immediately felt like that same awkward fifth-grader.

Why didn't things change with this new look?

Why didn't I feel any better than I did the year before?

I wouldn't get the answers to these questions until much later in my life, and that very point was the beginning of a long period for me—a period of confusion, low self-esteem, poor self-image, and negative thinking about myself.

Sometimes we search for exterior methods of validating our worth. We try all the latest diets, makeup and skin-care products, hairstyles, and fashion fads, yet we continue to come up empty. We do everything we can to not stand out or appear different from anyone else. Yet, even in our attempts to look like all the others, we still stand out.

Chosen from the Root

As I reflected on that time period, I figured out one very important point about myself. I was standing in my own way. The entire journey and the lessons learned were about *me*. The journey has been and is about moving *me* out of my own way and out of God's way so He could show me who I really am.

I was an extremely smart child, and I never had an issue with being smart because I always hung out with people who were smart too. I didn't worry about being teased for being smart. Just a side note: Most of the time, we find comfort and support when we're around like-minded individuals, people with the same mindset and spirit.

Mostly, all of my friends were extremely smart and focused on doing the best they could in school. Looking back, even though I thought I was the ugliest girl in the world, not everyone paid attention to my physical appearance. Sure, kids found reasons to tease me, but every kid got teased. For the most part, it was my character and personality that caused me to make friends easily, and I was even friends with some of the popular kids in school. At one point, I realized that I was popular in my own way. But to me, I was still *ugly!*

So, the message became clear (much later in life) that this low self-esteem wasn't something that was inflicted upon me by all of the "mean girls" or mean children who teased me and made my childhood miserable. I was doing this to myself. I was actually making myself miserable by wanting to shape my identity based on these superficial, unimportant physical qualities. Simply stated, I thought if I looked good, I'd feel good about myself, and looking good meant looking like everyone else. I didn't just want to be known as the smart girl; I wanted to be smart and beautiful and wanted boys to be attracted to me.

So much of what we (especially women) do to ourselves is motivated by how we see ourselves and, ultimately, the response we want from people. Consciously or subconsciously, this is the source of our lack of confidence. We have based our own self-esteem and confidence in how people see us. But the reality is that others usually don't see us the way we see ourselves, and God certainly doesn't see us the way we see ourselves! He sees us as His children, His creation, fearfully and wonderfully made in His likeness.

There's Purpose in the Roots

Just like the roots of our hair, our personal roots (where we've come from, who our family is, and how we were raised) play a part in our overall journey and growth. Just like our hair, new growth in our lives comes when the roots have been stimulated. When we pay attention to and confront our roots, we will become more aware of where we're going. There was no way I could even write this book and attempt to inspire and encourage you without taking a look back at where I've been. Reflecting on the past helps move us forward. It helps us grow. So often our growth is stunted because we are holding on to the negative ways in which we view ourselves (or have been told to view ourselves), the bad experiences from our past, or even guilt from the things we've done. We have to learn to be reflective of and grateful for the negative experiences because often those are the reasons we are so effective in helping other people; hence, these experiences help us find our purpose in life.

Also, as we reflect upon and shed the negativity of our past, we must learn how to see ourselves the way God sees us. If you are a believer, then you believe that God is the creator of the universe and all things in it. He created man and woman and gave us the ability to reproduce. Therefore, God created *you.* And since He created you, He then also gave you purpose.

There's nothing on this earth that is without a set purpose. And sometimes God chooses the most unlikely person to fulfill *greatness* for Him. Sure, He considers the roots of our journey, yet He still chooses to use us for a greater purpose. Why does He do this? He does this because He seeks out the heart and not physical appearance or other shallow, worldly measures of success and beauty.

I will give you an example, one of the most famous examples, of being chosen. God chose Mary, a young, poor virgin, to carry and bring forth life to His son, Jesus! To avoid the consequences of having a single-mother situation, He could've easily chosen a two-parent family with a kid and a donkey. (Did they have dogs back then?) But He didn't!

He *chose* Mary. It wasn't because of her education, her beauty, or her ability to capture the attention of lots of people when she entered a room. And it definitely wasn't because of how her hair was styled. God chose Mary because she loved Him more than anyone or anything else. He knew her heart, and the Bible says that He favored her! God recognized that she was open and willing to be used by Him. Can you believe that God actually based the carrying out of this special task on the amount of *love* she had for Him? What would happen if we loved God so much that He chose us to fulfill special tasks for Him? If we realized how much He wants to do through us, we would quickly learn how to really love God.

The Bible in Luke 1:29 says that when the angel Gabriel appeared to Mary, she was confused and disturbed (NLT). This isn't surprising. Sometimes we will experience periods—sometimes long periods—of confusion on our journey. But we should take Mary's example to heart. Even in the midst of confusion and doubt, she didn't stall or hesitate in accepting God's plan and purpose. We, like Mary, might be confused but also grateful for the opportunity to fulfill our God-given purpose. Mary accepted her purpose and knew that, in spite of her current situation or even her past, she was chosen to fulfill something monumental for her God. She knew that she wasn't really worthy of such an awesome responsibility. Nevertheless, she believed that what God said to her would be accomplished (Luke 1:45).

Our roots point us in the direction of our purpose in life. We can look at our past and start to understand what we were put on Earth to do. I now realize that my purpose in life is to glorify God by teaching, instructing, and empowering individuals and groups to live and be the best they can be. Because of my roots and the experiences I faced as a child who thought poorly of myself, I can relate to children, teens, and adults who deal with low self-esteem and who allow that low self-esteem to permeate every area of their lives. Since I have decided not to allow that low self-esteem to hinder me from walking out my purpose, I can teach others to do the same.

What experiences have you had in life that you have held on to as painful, hurtful experiences? If you take a look and consider that there was a purpose and a plan in all of it, it might help you start to figure out why parts of your life are without purpose. On a daily basis, I meet people who say that they have no clue what their purpose is in life. They don't know their God-given talents and abilities and/or how to use them to fulfill their divine assignment. Usually, I end up listening to them talk about their past and some of the things they've experienced in life (people tend to connect with me and feel comfortable talking to me about their problems, issues, and challenges). So often, I end up pointing them in the direction of looking at those experiences and figuring out how they are impacting their lives at that very moment. Instead of looking at them as problems or issues, I urge them to view those negative actions as opportunities to find purpose. There are so many examples in the Bible where God used a negative situation to bring about a greater purpose. God allows certain things to occur in our lives for several reasons. I believe God desires to get our attention in some situations. But in other situations, I believe God wants *us* to know who we are, how strong He created us, and what our purpose is while we're here on earth.

QUESTIONS TO CONSIDER:

1. What do your roots say about who you are?

2. What have you identified as your purpose in life?

3. How are you cultivating your roots to make sure that they help and not hinder you walking in your purpose?

4. What negative experiences from your past are you holding on to that are hindering you from fulfilling your dreams, goals, and purpose?

5. How do you plan to let go of those experiences and use them to show you how to help others?

Lifesaver Two:
Growth Is an Intentional Process

I've given you some basic background information about my roots and where all the feelings of low self-esteem and negative self-image began. If you find yourself stuck, or in a negative frame of mind about yourself and who you are, then you, too, need to begin to reflect on your roots. Proper reflection on the past will always bring you to the present with the insight to move forward.

Once you've observed, studied, and reflected on your roots, there now has to be a commitment to growth. Because if we continue to focus only on the past and where we've been, we'll never begin to look toward our future and where we need to go. So we have to make the *decision* to grow. And while we never completely forget about our past, we have to look and move forward. Part of looking forward is to begin to understand how and why we make decisions. The reason it's important to look at our decision-making is so that we won't repeat the same mistakes in life over and over again. Sometimes, situations in life cause us to make various choices. At times, those choices get us into situations that were never intended for us. We get stuck in a place because we get into the pattern of making similar choices. It's important to know our patterns and the events, logic, emotions, and experiences that guide our decision-making so we can move forward.

Decisions Should Be Intentional

The word *decision* evokes a sense of fear and anxiety in many people. For many, it symbolizes finality and a conclusion that might be scary to a person who is fearful of its consequences. Someone recently told me that making decisions feels like standing at the edge of a cliff. Every possible consequence from that decision might mean something different and affect different people.

However, whether or not you are fearful of making decisions, it is inevitable that at many points in your life you will be forced to make a decision. Every day we are faced with the huge task of making decisions—from simple to more difficult ones. We have to decide what to wear, what to eat, what to drink, even where to park our car. While those may represent some of the easier decisions, there are also more important decisions we face on a daily basis—decisions like where to send our children to day care or school, whether to accept or quit a job, or whether to remain in a marriage or seek a divorce.

We are spiritual beings created by God who are also given the power of free will. So, as spiritual and human beings, we have the privilege of choosing what we want to do with our lives on a daily basis. However, even in our decision-making process, sometimes, we make unconscious decisions. We make the choice to do or not do certain things, and often that choice is influenced by some negative emotion or event that has occurred in our lives.

There was a period in my life when I felt like I was just going through the motions, making decisions "just because." I had a negative view of who I was as a young woman and really didn't feel too great about myself. Regardless of what others said to or about me, I just didn't feel good about myself. I wanted to be thinner, prettier, lighter, taller, smarter, more popular, less conservative, and more fun. In my mind, I just wasn't good enough. Even though I had not figured out what I wasn't good enough for, it was still a feeling of inadequacy. So, like many young women with poor self-esteem and low self-confidence, I looked for that validation from exterior sources, even from my parents.

Before I discuss some of my experiences, mistakes, and lessons learned as an adolescent and young woman, I'd like to take a moment to discuss self-esteem. We throw this word around so often, and it's important for me to define my use of the word in hopes that you will see why I can attribute my journey to it or the lack thereof. My personal view of myself became a barrier for me. And since my hope is that you will develop an appreciation of who you are and why you were placed here, I think it's important that we discuss this concept of self-esteem.

A few definitions of *self-esteem* that I found helpful and interesting were 1) from *The McGraw-Hill Concise Dictionary of Modern Medicine*, which defines self-esteem as "the internalized sense of one's own worth" and 2) from *Mosby's Dental Dictionary*, which defines it as "the degree of worth and competence one attributes to oneself."

However, for the purposes of this book, I would like to use the following as my definition of low self-esteem:

A hatred of the true self; an unwillingness to accept the self for who it is and embrace all the unique qualities one possesses.

When someone has a low sense of self-worth, it really means that they hate who they really are or who they think they really are. Often the reason we have low self-esteem is we don't know who we are. And other times, it's because we don't accept who we are and choose to hate the true self.

Regardless, low self-esteem manifests in many ways. Low self-esteem can sometimes look like anger, depression, apathy, sexual promiscuity, an attempt at isolation or seclusion, the constant need for sociability, and the list goes on. I can honestly say that I suffered from the disease of low self-esteem for most of my life (childhood to my twenties). There were times when I was a teenager that I really wanted to not "live" anymore because I felt I was so ugly and that no boy would ever like me. I'm not talking about suicide. I'm talking about not having a desire to truly *live*. I didn't want to make friends, go to sleepovers, talk to people on the phone, join clubs and groups, or interact with people. And it was because I wasn't thin, I didn't have long hair, my face was full of acne, I wore thick glasses, and my hair was nappy!

The worst thing was when I turned seventeen and people began to comment on how beautiful I was. All I could think about was that I felt like the ugliest *thing* in the world. And, as an adolescent, those thoughts stayed with me throughout young adulthood. I remember the first boy that ever liked me. I couldn't believe it. As a matter of fact, I didn't believe it. I thought he was playing a mean joke on me, and I actually cried because I was hurt that someone could be so cruel. But he actually liked me. And I didn't even know how to accept that. He thought I was "cute," and he wanted to get to know me, but because of how I saw myself, I couldn't receive his kindness.

The Decision to Pretend

So, as I began to blossom into a young woman, those feelings of self-hatred and the expression of that low self-esteem became more apparent through my decisions. There was a period of my life, during college, where I started to gain a false sense of confidence based on the approval of men. I began to get compliments about my physical appearance and attributes, and it made me feel "good" about myself. When I would receive compliments, for a brief moment I felt beautiful. However, there's something about the mind and the spirit. You can walk around and pretend to be what you're not and do things that aren't in line with who you are or how you feel, and it will begin to wear you out. *It takes a lot of effort to pretend.* So, for a while, there was a period of promiscuity in my relationships and interactions with men. I used their attraction and attention to feel what I needed to feel emotionally. The brief sexual attention and attraction from men was all a temporary way to feel better about myself. I wanted desperately to love myself. I figured that since I didn't love myself, why not at least let someone else love me?

As I reflect, what has been so disappointing is realizing that I hadn't even been raised to feel that way about myself. My parents were strong Christian believers who taught me who I was in the sight of God, and they showered me with love and attention. They supported me and encouraged me to find myself and be all I could be. They taught me that I could do all things through Christ, who was my strength, and my mom (a strong woman) let me know that I was beautiful and created in the image of God. But somehow it didn't register with me. I allowed the teasing from my childhood and the need to be accepted according to worldly standards of beauty to define me and who I would become.

My need and desire to be accepted and please other people was so strong and intense that I denied myself the opportunity to discover who I really was, just to fit in. Recently, I was watching a movie that was released in 2003 called *What a Girl Wants*, and there was a line in the movie that stood out as I wrote this book. The main character's boyfriend asked her a question: "Why are you trying so hard to fit in when you were meant to stand out?"

I didn't understand where I belonged because my low sense of self-worth had created a specific personality for me. I felt that I had to fit the image of the person who I wanted to be, and as a result, I conformed. I conformed to the image of the people who I closely identified with and who I wanted to be just like. I changed my hair, style of dress, speech, and even developed certain friendships and relationships in order to become the person I wanted to become.

As I think about pretending and trying to fit in where I didn't belong, I am reminded of an analogy from a message I heard from Bishop T. D. Jakes called "The Witness of Change." In that message, he talked about how people try to put puzzles together, and they have all the pieces but sometimes they want to finish the puzzle so badly that they start trying to stick pieces into spaces where they don't fit. And no matter how much they try to force that piece into that space, it won't stay. It will always pop out because that's not the space that piece was designed for. Similarly, as people we sometimes try to fit into spaces, circles, groups, organizations, and crowds that we are not meant to fit into. And every time we do that, we won't remain there; we keep popping out because we don't belong in that space.

Decisions Serve a Purpose— Even the "Long" Ones

So, the point is, we have to make decisions throughout our lives. Sometimes we make decisions that have positive consequences and sometimes we make decisions that have negative consequences in our lives. However, I am a believer that whatever decision we make, it will ultimately serve its purpose. The power of choice is a strong force in our lives. We have the ability to choose our own path, and we have the ability to decide how we will live our lives. I don't even feel comfortable saying we make "wrong" decisions. I believe we make "long" decisions—and by this I mean that there are decisions that take us the "long route" to our destiny. Some of our decisions are like detours on our journey. But even during a detour we see something we wouldn't have seen if we had taken the preferred route.

Decisions Change Your Life: For Better and for Worse

In 2003, at the young age of twenty-three, I made the decision to get married. I wasn't forced or coerced to get married at such a young age. I share this part of my life as a way to give insight on how we allow our self-esteem and lack of self-confidence to guide our decisions, and sometimes we aren't even aware that this is what's happening. I'm not saying that twenty-three is too young an age to get married, in general (although I don't really believe that one really knows himself or herself fully at age twenty-three), but I am saying that for *me* it was *too* young.

Sometimes we can be in such a specific place in our own emotional and spiritual lives that we attract the very person we are at that time. We attract people who are in the same place, spiritually and emotionally. And we turn what was meant to be a seasonal relationship into a long-term commitment. I don't in any way intend to shine a negative light on the man I married, and if he ever reads this, I hope he doesn't take offense to it. These are truths about that time and experience in my life that

I'm using to help others who might find themselves in the same or similar position.

I am a helper. I often feel bad for people and want to help make their lives better. I feel so blessed to have had such a wonderful family that raised me and gave me opportunities. So, because of that, I want to share my experiences with others who were not as fortunate. In a way, it makes me feel good to help others experience new things and encourage them to reach their goals. So, I met a man who became a friend, and he was someone who I thought needed my help. In fact, I felt that he needed me in order to make his life better. In hindsight (which we know is always 20/20), he didn't need my help at all. My problem was that I didn't know who I was. I had just graduated from college, and I felt like I'd lived as a "girl gone wild" for four years. (I realize now that I was just being a "normal" college student.)

But after college, I was ready to begin my life as a responsible adult—one who went to work, had social time with friends, attended church on Sundays, and lived "normally." What I needed was balance in my life and my heart, but I didn't know how to reach that. When I met him, he was someone who treated me with kindness and respect, so I thought he must be the man I'm meant to marry, right? Boy, was I clueless! How could I marry someone and be with him the rest of my life when I didn't even know who I was? Needless to say, at the young age of twenty-three, I was very confused and didn't understand that the type of man I attracted then was because of who I was at the time. (Side note: We attract who we are.) If, back then, I had developed and matured into the true, natural self that God created, I wouldn't have made the decision to get married at that point in my life—especially to someone with whom I was never truly *in love* (not to mention we only knew each other a year before getting engaged). If I were texting right now, I'd type *SMH* (Shaking My Head).

The woman God created me to be is bold, confident, secure, strong, balanced, and beautiful. She would've decided to spend more time determining if the emotions associated with the relationship were based on true compatibility, love, affection, and principles rather than on a lack of self-confidence and poor self-image. She would've chosen to marry a man who would allow her the freedom to be herself and be comfortable and secure enough to be okay with her without trying to change her.

But I did it. I got married, and for five years I lived with a man who, to this day, doesn't really know *me*. That is partly my fault because I never exposed him to the real me. As I discovered who I was as a woman, I kept her a secret from him. I think I knew that he wouldn't accept and love the real me. So after many years of trying to please him and be who he wanted me to be, I couldn't pretend anymore. It took way too much energy to pretend. I had begun to move farther away from my own purpose and destiny just to try to give a false sense of confidence and security to an insecure person. As I started to mature, and as my relationship with God grew, I started becoming more aware of the woman I was and the man I'd married. And those two people didn't belong together.

During my marriage, I started to truly learn about myself. I began to understand why I thought the way I did, acted the way I did, moved the way I did, laughed the way I did, cried the way I did, and loved the way I did. For the first time in my life, I started to love myself. Then, I inwardly discovered that what I expected for my life and from my husband was not unreasonable and that it was founded on true principles. I've never claimed to have been the "perfect wife" (if there is such a thing). I did and said things that I shouldn't have, and I treated him with a lack of respect at times. I understand now that I was trying to figure out how to be myself in a marriage to a man who wasn't secure enough to be okay with who I really was.

I started to pray for a change. I started getting closer to God and asking Him who I was and how to relate better to my husband. On the surface, I wanted it to work, but deep in my heart I wanted out—and that's me being honest with you. I knew what he couldn't handle. He wasn't someone who would make me a better, more open person. He would only keep me in my shell and smother my purpose. What I began to realize about my marriage is that we joined ourselves together and forced a spiritual connection that was more based on church, the concept of "right and wrong," and the opinions of others instead of a true emotional and spiritual connection based on love and the principles of God.

Spiritual connection isn't based on the fact that you both go to the same church or even believe in the same God; it is based on the divine connection of hearts, minds, and spirits through the common understanding of values, dreams, desires, principles, and an innate ability to love without conditions.

Once I figured this out, I began to focus on my personal growth through my relationship with God.

QUESTIONS TO CONSIDER:

1. What do your past decisions say about who you are right now?

2. What do your current decisions say about where you are in your life?

3. How can you align your decision-making with where you are going?

4. Are you living with regret about decisions you've made in your past? If so, how can you begin to let go and move forward?

5. How is God reaching out to you help you make better decisions?

Lifesaver Three:
In Order to Grow, Change Is Not Optional

So, at age twenty-eight, I knew something needed to change. I was actively growing and pursuing my relationship with God, yet many things in my life remained the same. I've had to make many decisions throughout my life. And what I've come to realize is that the future depends on what we do in the present. I don't always use a formal theoretical approach to decision-making, but it is definitely important for me to make informed decisions. It is imperative that I gather information and weigh the options (count the costs, so to speak) so that I can make the best decision for *me*.

Ultimately, the decision was that I needed change. Some things in my life had to change. If everything in our life is consistently the same, that's usually a sign that not much growth is occurring in our life. In order to grow, we must be willing to change (and shift) through life. At that time, I began to think of some significant things I could do to start changing my life. But nothing seemed real enough to bring about any real change. Then, I began to read the Bible more and slowly started to understand the principles of God much more. It was as if the words on the page became *life* for me. God was drawing me closer to Him and revealing His purpose for my life, through the understanding of some extremely important principles in His word. I started seeing things and people in a different light. I started viewing myself in a different light. I saw everything in a different light. I remembered that I was chosen by God for something important, and I began to live like I was chosen instead of living like I didn't want the life I had. The Word of God became a "lamp unto my feet and a light unto my path" (Psalm 119:105).

Transition—Breakage—Change

In August 2008, I remember going to get a relaxer in my hair for a wedding of an in-law's, and little did I know this would be my last relaxer. Shortly after that relaxer, I decided to just grow out my hair and take it from there. I hadn't really *decided* to go natural, but I knew I wanted to do something different with my hair. One evening, in December 2008, I was sitting on the sofa in my living room surfing the Internet, and I was searching the word *transitioning*. I ended up on a very popular natural hair site (Nappturality.com) and read an article that explained the process of transitioning. I remember reading about how the process involves patience and how there will be mixed emotions while you transition your hair. The article stated that you could go from fear to frustration and excitement to elation over the course of four to six weeks. But then I read the following part, and I immediately connected with it and *knew* that going natural was for me.

> When you relax your hair, you change its natural attributes to the opposite of what they are. You have changed the coiliest of hair to the straightest of hair (depending, of course, on how straight your relaxed hair is). The line where these two textures meet is called the *line of demarcation*. This is the weakest part of a hair strand. The two textures fight against each other at this point, causing a weak point where they meet. This is where the hair breaks off. (www. napturality.com)

I connected with this part so much because when I "relaxed" my hair, I was ultimately denying my true natural self. Remember from Lifesaver Two where I discussed my definition of low self-esteem as the hatred of the true self. When I wore my hair relaxed and straight, I was changing who I really was to be someone who I really wasn't. I felt like I was pretending. But from this transitioning process, I would be able to go through the phases of changing back to who I really was, back to myself. It wouldn't be an abrupt, sudden change, but it would be a *slow growth and acceptance* of the true Margaret. God wanted to transform me by changing the way I thought about myself, His purpose for me, and my life. I thought about what Paul wrote in Romans 12:2, where he stated, "Don't copy the behavior and customs of this world, but let God transform you into a new person by changing the way you think. Then you will learn to know God's will for you, which is good and pleasing and perfect" (NLT).

My new mind and new life would begin with this hair journey. As I sat on the sofa and read the article and thought about the experience I would embark upon, I began to cry. They were tears of joy, fear, anticipation, worry, doubt, and all other emotions in between. I was mostly afraid of and excited by the possibilities. I knew that if God had revealed this to me, that meant there was a great blessing ahead. Not necessarily a tangible one, like we often look for, but a spiritual one.

I was afraid. I didn't know what to expect. But I was willing to drop my idea of what needed to happen in my life for what God wanted me to do with it.

Mark 8:35 states, "If you try to hang on to your life, you will lose it. But if you give up your life for my sake and for the sake of the Good News, you will save it" (NLT).

I was ready to let go. I wanted God to do something new and different in my life. So, I was *willing* to obey for the sake of being able to share His goodness with you. But I was still afraid. *Fear*! Whew . . . this is a word that I deal with every day. I recognize its potential power, so I fight it by believing the opposite of what *it* tells me. So many times in our lives, fear settles in and makes us believe that we won't be able to go through that which we've been called to. As fear slowly creeps into every area of our lives, it cripples us. Fear causes us to stand still when we need to move. Fear causes us to give up when we should keep going. Fear keeps us holding on to things and people we should let go of. Fear makes us believe that we will be inadequate, that we will fail and not survive. Fear speaks to that very part of us that we keep secret from even our closest friends and family. Fear settles into the places in our hearts that are dark, cold, and lonely and rests there. Fear is contrary to hope, assurance, confidence, faith, and love.

There is a passage of Scripture that says "Such love has no fear because perfect love expels all fear. If we are afraid, it is for punishment, and this shows that we have not fully experienced his perfect love. We love each other because he loved us first" (1 John 4:18–19 NLT).

This is exciting news for those who are afraid of anything and everything. This means that as we face fear, it's important to recognize that the way to combat or fight fear is to believe and walk in God's love. He loves us, so there is nothing to fear. It's a comfort to know that his perfect love drives out all fear and that as we fully experience His love for us, we will go through life free from fear. As we get to know Him and His plans for us (remember that Jeremiah 29:11 says his plans are not to harm us), we begin to realize how wide and deep and long and high his love is for us, and that there's nothing we can do to separate from that love. We then start to walk without fear. Because, as the Scripture says, his love is perfect and it expels (drives out, casts out) fear!

I'm not, and have never been, what I call a "spooky spiritual," which in my definition is one who thinks God sits up on high, controlling and enforcing our every move with his hand, like a puppet master. I do, though, believe that the Holy Spirit is a guide. When we accept him into our lives, he places his spirit within us and leads and guides us to make the best decisions for our lives, if we listen. He also helps prepare us for our purpose and gives us the strength to carry out our calling. The hair journey, *my* hair journey, was inspired by the Holy Spirit.

So, the hair journey for me would be a journey of *transformation*, and I would be totally and completely changed as a result. Not to mention, the next two years of my life would be the most scary, interesting, embarrassing, humiliating, and hurtful time in my life. I believe that the Spirit knew what needed to be placed within me (heart, mind, and soul) in order to endure what I would soon face.

God Was in My Hair

In 2009, I experienced a situation in my marriage that would've shaken a lot of women from their foundation and struck them to the very core of their soul. But because God was in my hair, he prepared and fortified me from the outside in. He prepped me for the mess—I can't think of any better word to describe it—I would endure. For the purposes of this book, I have chosen not to go into detail about the specific situations, within my marriage, that caused me hurt and pain. There were so many different elements that it would literally take another book to share all the details. However, I don't think you really need the details to understand what I'm saying. We all have our own "story" with all the gory, intimate details that would be a blockbuster hit for directors like Tyler Perry, complete with the "crying and praying and singing all at the same time" scene.

Now, you might be thinking, what in the world is she talking about? God was in her hair? Lord, have mercy, she's lost it. And, before I made this journey, I'd probably agree with you. But since I stepped into this new realm of understanding how who I am directly relates to how I deal with situations in my life, it's not strange to me that He took something so seemingly meaningless as hair and created a platform by which to save my life.

God's message to me was that I was prepared for this storm (and the ones that would follow) because I was obedient to what God was trying to do in *me* through my hair journey/ spiritual transformation. During the process, I stepped back, for the first time in my life, to think clearly and look at the situation with my heart and make the best decision for myself. I will remind you that I'd already come to the realization that I was not with the right man and that I desired change. So, *my* decision was to divorce. Uh-oh! I think I just lost a few of you. I think I just lost you because I just heard you say, "No, no, no. She's professing to be a Christian, but she got a divorce." And my response to you is, "Yes, and unapologetically."

At that time in my life, there were so many confusing messages being given to me. Christian leaders were telling me that I needed to stay and work things out and that my marriage would be an example to many. Others were saying, "Well, Jesus gave permission to divorce in cases of infidelity." However, all I knew is that I wanted out. That's as honest as I can be. And, if my husband were to admit it, he wanted out too. So, just so you won't put the book down and stop reading, let me pause here and say that as a believer of Christ, I do not advocate divorce. And in no way am I saying that God told me to leave my husband. I am definitely aware of the spiritual, emotional, and financial consequences of ending a marriage. And in marriages where there is love, companionship, mutual understanding, a true spiritual connection, and resilience, I would advocate for a couple to seek professional help and try to work things out. Ultimately, the heartache and pain caused by divorce isn't worth it, if both people want to save the marriage.

But in my case, I wanted to be *free* from a marriage that was turning me into a person no one recognized—not even my family. I didn't want to be free to be wild and have random sexual affairs with different men—that is what many would call *loose*, not free. But I realized that I couldn't live the balanced life that I was designed to live and be with him too. I couldn't dream big and set goals for myself. I would've had to accept a life prescribed for me by my husband, our church leaders, his family, and I really wouldn't have lived in total spiritual, emotional, and mental freedom. My family and friends all told me later that they didn't ever know me as that married person. They never saw me as that person. They knew I wasn't truly being myself, and they were worried that I'd lost myself in the marriage. They were partly right.

As I look back on that time in my life, I realize that I didn't *lose* myself; I made the choice to hide my true self out of fear and complacency. I didn't want my husband to continue to tell me how much I needed to be different or not do this and not do that. So I became who he wanted me to be. I wore my hair straight, wore no makeup, went to work every day, came home, sat around and watched television, went to Bible study on Wednesdays and church on Sundays, and spent time with his family. Occasionally, there was a short vacation to the beach. But other than that, every day, every week, every month, and every year was the same. I fell into the "comfort zone" of marriage and developed a façade to make sure that people thought I was happy. But deep within myself I was very uncomfortable, very unhappy, and in bondage. The real me was hidden deep inside and wanted to be free to live, laugh, cry, make mistakes, spend time with friends, travel and see other places, try new foods, meet new people, develop new friendships, and soar!

My divorce was more about setting my spirit free and going back to who God created me to be and less about leaving a horrible man. To this day, there are positives that came from my marriage and being with my ex-husband. We were both young and made many mistakes, but I know that because of my marriage I am a much stronger, mature woman, and I now have an idea of what my ideal marriage looks like and the type of man I *need* in my life.

Accept Change; Move Forward

I would be a liar if I sat here and wrote that accepting all the changes in life is easy. It most certainly isn't easy. Change means that things in your life won't be the same. It means that the good times you had will simply be memories from the past, and those moments will never return. Change means realizing that some relationships and friendships will end. There is a certain feeling of loss and grief that comes with divorce (or the end of a relationship). When a marriage ends, it is somewhat like a death. But a divorce doesn't have to mean a total spiritual and emotional death. Divorce represents a death that is calling out for some area of your life to live. As with any relationship that isn't healthy for you, there comes a time when you have to break away in order to live.

There are three very important parts to accepting change that I would like to share with you. You can think of these as steps to accepting change. If you think about these as steps, you can start to see how various situations in your life are still calling for you to accept the change they brought.

1. *Wake up and pay attention*: Sometimes we cannot accept change because we don't recognize that what is going on around us is causing a shift or change in our lives. Benjamin Franklin once stated, "The definition of insanity is doing the same thing over and over and expecting different results." If we continue to do things that cause us pain and draw us away from God and expect our lives to change, we might be suffering from periods of insanity. If it's not working, wake up and recognize that it's not working. If what we want in life isn't in line with what we're doing to get there, then it's time to change directions. But we don't know we're going in the wrong direction if we haven't been paying attention. As an example, think about a GPS navigational system in your car and how you depend on it to get somewhere. Let's say you started the GPS and the voice is guiding you to your destination. All of a sudden you get a phone call, and you become

so engrossed in the conversation that you stop paying attention to the GPS. Well, when you get off the phone, you notice that the GPS voice is continuously saying, "Recalculating . . ." because it's trying to get you back on track. You now realize that you're going the wrong way, and you start paying attention again to get back on track. This happens in our lives too. We get distracted from where we're really going and the journey that will take us there. Sometimes we have detours that take us off course, but if we start paying attention, we will hear a voice saying, "Recalculating . . ." and it is a voice within our spirit that wants to guide us to get us back on track.

2. *Seek counsel:* When you are on the brink of a major life change, major disappointment or failure, or just feeling low and in need of a jump start, it helps to gain other perspectives. Isolating yourself is dangerous. Trust me. It's not wise to sit at home in the dark listening to Sade with a bottle of wine, drinking your sorrows away. Because the reality is, when the "two-buck chuck" is gone, the problems are still there. It is easy to slip into depression when you are going through major life changes. Sometimes the changes aren't as drastic as a divorce, but even if it's something like losing your job, having problems with your children, or just a general sense of unhappiness, it's important to be around other

people—positive people who love you. Human nature is sometimes contrary to this because we just want to be alone to "sort it all out." And I believe that there is validity in spending time alone and in meditation and reflection. But I can also attest to the wonderful feeling of having people in your life you can call, ask questions of, and just get some wisdom from. Others have experienced what you are going through, and while we all have our *own* story and the feelings that come with it, sometimes it's a familiar story to someone else. I believe that we experience things in life in order to help someone else. God places people in our lives who will support us and help us process our feelings. Sometimes our feelings and emotions will bind us and prevent us from moving forward. We have to address and deal with our emotions, but at some point we have to line up our emotions with what God says about us and where we're going. Jeremiah 29:11 says " 'For I know the plans I have for you,' says the Lord. 'They are plans for good and not for disaster, to give you a future and a hope' " (NLT). But sometimes we start feeling like there is no hope and nothing in our future to look forward to. So when we seek counsel from one of our supporters or those who are placed in our lives to help us, we will start to remember what God says about us. We will gain more joy, and in that joy we will find strength (Nehemiah 8:10).

3. *Make a plan*: I know you probably weren't expecting that to be the third step. But it is! In life, it's important to plan. Many people are confused about how to plan and still live and walk by faith in God. As we go through life, our reliance on God and His power in our lives becomes the basis for everything else in our lives. So as we walk with Him and in His will, He will lead and guide us. However, God has given us something that is so awesome and powerful. He gave us the ability to dream, desire, and choose. So, as we walk with Him, we can have dreams and visions, and then we can decide to go after them. He is still involved in this process because we must ask Him to bless our dreams and plans. But as we prepare for major changes in life, there are some things that need to be planned.

For example, if you decide to take a trip or vacation, you don't just go to the airport and pray for God to move. You go online and do research about prices for flights, hotels, and other activities that you might want to do while you're on your vacation. Then, if you already have the money, you book the trip. If you don't, you set a plan to save for the vacation so you can book the trip later. Then, you begin planning for activities, transportation from the airport, and what clothes you will take with you. There is planning that goes into it.

So why would you go through something as *huge* as your *life* without a plan!?

After my divorce, I started thinking about what my next steps would be; as a result, I immediately started planning. I knew there had to be a purpose that would come out of all of my heartache and mistakes. This book was a part of that plan. I knew that I needed to pen this experience and journey for others. I started my blog, www.spirituallynatural.com, as a way to capture the many lessons that were coming from the journey and the pain. As you face a current change or shift in your life, make a plan. Write the vision and make it plain. There are things you want to accomplish. Write them down and make a plan to get them done. And ask God to bless the plan. Ask Him to lead you and guide you in your planning process. He will do it. Sometimes God isn't expecting you to wait for Him; he's actually waiting for you to act.

If you start with these three steps, you will begin to receive more clarity about how to move forward in life. You will start to activate some principles in your life that are definite tools for success and growth. What is it you are afraid of? Think about how fear might play into your ability to move forward. Think about the worst that could happen if you don't make it. If you don't make it, you will die with a dream unfulfilled. That's the only thing you should fear. So, other than that, you will make mistakes. You will feel like you don't know what you're doing and where you're going, but keep walking. Keep moving. Keep planning and replanning. There are times when we do not move forward because we are unsure of the direction that God wants us to go. However, even as we follow a course in life and somehow end up on the wrong path, God will convict us and give clear instructions to change directions. It takes a listening ear to hear His voice and an obedient spirit to follow His direction.

QUESTIONS TO CONSIDER:

1. Identify ways that God is trying to get your attention about your life.

2. What transition process are you going through or have you gone through that has shifted or changed your outlook about your life?

3. What strategies can you employ to begin realizing some real growth in your life?

4. In what areas of your life are you longing to experience spiritual and emotional freedom?

5. What can you do to start experiencing freedom in your life?

How My Hair Saved My Life

By now you're probably wondering, "When is she going to explain how her hair saved her life?" Well, I've been telling you all along about my hair journey and how it was an outward experience that symbolized inner changes. Now I will share the specific lessons that my hair journey has taught me along the way. These lessons represent how God changed my life through this natural hair journey. As it happened, I was able to look at my life in a totally different way; hence, I was able to make decisions that saved my life. My hair saved my life. God saved my life, because through my hair He saved me from a spiritual death. The pain, torment, heartache, embarrassment, and ridicule I faced would have killed my free, loving spirit. Instead, through my hair, I gained the strength I needed to endure and continue living and loving. God showed me that

I am indeed free. He let me know that when I gave my life to Him, He truly set me free. But it is up to me (and you) to accept that freedom. Freedom doesn't mean doing whatever you want to do; freedom means that you have the room and space in which to live, make mistakes, love, laugh, experience joy and pain, and still know that God is right there with you.

I am still on this journey of new growth, so I'm sure that more revelations are on their way. And I'm sure there will be more books after this one! I want to share my first few "I-openers" and revelatory lessons with you as brief affirmations with the hope that you will read them, connect with their message, and begin speaking positively to yourself as you travel on your own journey. My ultimate hope is that you will embrace whatever is your own journey and see it as a way to be transformed, renewed, and restored.

I Am Free!

It was close to the end of writing this book when I finally "got" this message. It almost made me change the title of my book, but the title I'd chosen still fit, ironically. I was thinking about my hair journey and how much change I'd gone through during the past few years. Also, I began to think about the stressful uncertainty of my future and the status of my current financial well-being (unemployed, struggling to start a business, having barely enough to make ends meet). But then I thought about the beautiful friends and family members in my life. I had a wonderful set of parents who were supportive of my dreams, gave me counsel when I needed it, and were able to speak positive encouragement into my life at the right times. I had a great brother, sister-in-law, and niece who cheered up my day whenever I saw them. I had a very special friend who always knew exactly what to say to lift my spirits and let me know that I had help and support. And I even had friends going through similar trials who pooled resources together with me to have a wonderful Memorial Day cookout!

Then it dawned on me. Recently, I was driving down the street alone, and I ended up shouting out loud, "But I'm free!" It was like fifty million fireworks had shot off in my heart and mind at that very moment. I had been writing this book and trying to explain this concept of how, through my hair journey, my life had been saved and spared. I had been trying to convey the essence of how I felt when I began living as my natural self. So, at that time, I finally knew how to explain it. This journey was, and still is, about *freedom*!

I again read John 8:36 in the New Living Translation, and as I read it, I literally had a "duh" moment! It was like it read, "Margaret, so if the Son sets you free, then you are truly free, DUH!" I don't in any way mean to reduce the Scriptures to such simple terms; however, I believe that when we are able to read the Scriptures and apply them to our personal lives and/ or situations, they will become *life* to us. That's what it meant to me—it meant that through this journey, I would experience new life, new growth, and freedom. Sure, I'd been a believer for years, and I even grew up the daughter of a pastor, with parents who taught me the way. However, it wasn't until I embarked upon this journey in my life that I understood what true spiritual freedom really was. Let me try to explain a little further what I really mean.

For a period of about eighteen years, I chemically altered my God-given hair. I relaxed it to make it straight because that's the way I thought it should be based on the way others wore their hair or liked my hair. I didn't embrace myself as God really created me to be. I didn't really know who I was, and honestly, I didn't want to know. I wanted to blend in with everyone else through my looks, speech, dress, and behavior.I longed to be accepted based on all the wrong qualities. The important qualities were less important to me, and I chose not to focus on those as a way to connect with or relate to people. This practice wasn't just present in the way I wore my hair but was present in everything that I did. I was a "people pleaser." I always worried about making sure that I did exactly what was expected of me and tried never to veer off the comfortable, compliant path.

I believe that, foundationally, I was taught very sound life principles. But other than that, my life was mine to live. However, I allowed everyone else to dictate how I should live my life. I definitely made choices, but most of my choices were influenced by what I considered might be other people's potential reactions to my choices instead of choosing to follow my heart. And for a long time I rebelled against what was best for me, simply because I was tired of doing what everyone wanted me to do. But one thing this journey has taught me is that I am who I am. I cannot change the things about me that make me unique and individual.

Constantly thinking about how others see you, or how they think you should present yourself through your physical appearance, is similar to being in bondage. You are bound to the opinions and desires of others, and bondage is deeply rooted in fear. Wherever fear is present, one cannot truly be free. When you are bound, you are constantly worried about (and afraid of) what will happen if you go against what others expect. Will people accept me? Will my family understand that this is really who I am? Will my friends shun me for being different?

I Am Who I Am and I Am Beautiful!

My self-esteem as a child, adolescent, and young woman was so contrary to this first affirmation. Looking back on my childhood, I can honestly say that my view of myself was horrible. I was a wreck! My self-esteem made me believe that I was ugly and there was nothing beautiful about me. But when I decided to transition from my relaxed hair to my natural hair, I began to look at myself in a totally different light. I went through an uncomfortable phase (some call it an "ugly phase") with my hair in which I didn't know what to do with it. I wanted it to be straight, but it wouldn't straighten like it did when there was a relaxer in it. I started going to get blowouts (straightening natural hair with heat instead of chemicals) at a local salon, and the stylist would straighten it. She was an amazing stylist, and I was so happy with the results when she would straighten it. But even with her incredible skills, my hair would still only be silky straight for a few days, for as soon as the North Carolina humidity got to it, it would go back to its natural state. During that phase of the journey, I still had an unwillingness to accept the kinky, curly hair that was growing in, so I kept getting blowouts.

There finally came a point in the journey when I started looking at my hair and paying attention to it. My hair began to grow so quickly. This growth was symbolic of the growth in my spiritual and emotional life. I then realized that I had to embrace it and learn how to work with it and manage it. I could no longer try to hide it or cover it up. It was my hair. It was me. And I was beautiful that way. Beauty took on a new definition for me. Beauty wasn't only referring to my physical features, but the word began to describe my spiritual qualities. As I began to think about my definition of beauty, the following definition from Dictionary.com resonated with me:

Beauty: The quality present in a thing or person that gives intense pleasure or deep satisfaction to the mind, whether arising from sensory manifestations (as shape, color, sound, etc.), a meaningful design or pattern, or something else (as in a personality in which high spiritual qualities are manifest).

My view of myself is no longer based on society's standard of beauty. I have a more spiritual, inward basis for beauty. I would rather be happy with myself than be concerned with what others think of me. I would rather my definition of beauty stem from God's view of who I am as a person than from a worldly standard of outward beauty based on the most "beautiful" celebrities. Of course, there are still things about myself that I would like to change, but I now have a new attitude about why and how to change those things. However, now as I wear my natural styles (twist-outs, braid-outs, soft curly 'fros, cornrows, pony puffs, twists), I have a newfound confidence.

What does God say about me (us) and who I am (we are)? God sees me, and all of us, as His children. The Bible says— and I believe it—that He created us in His own image. And in Psalm 139, David praises God for his being fearfully and wonderfully made (which was going to be the title of my first book, had I not experienced this hair journey). I think David felt the way I felt. I think David realized how awesome God must really be to create such creatures as us. That everything about us—our complexities, our physical appearance, our abilities, our voices.—were all created by our Lord. David wrote: "For you created my inmost being; you knit me together in my mother's womb. I praise you because I am fearfully and wonderfully made; your works are wonderful, I know that full well" (Psalm 139:13–14 NIV).

You, too, are beautiful. You have been given a unique personality, character, and physical appearance that were meant to be appreciated and celebrated.

Why do we continue to allow society's standard of beauty and acceptance to drive us to make decisions about how we wear our hair, dress, or feel about ourselves? I do not shun women who do not wear their hair in a natural state. Neither do I look upon those who wear natural hair as women who "have it all together," emotionally. Whatever we decide to do in terms of our physical appearance should be rooted in a personal appreciation of who we are and not based on who we want to look like. Even if you begin wearing your hair naturally, it should be because you have made the decision to do so for your own personal reasons and not because it is becoming a fad or trend.

I Am Strong

Merriam-Webster's definition of strength is "the power to resist force; the power of resisting attack." My decision to go back to my natural hair was motivated by the desire to build up the physical strength of my hair, but also to build emotional and spiritual strength within me. Hair is always strongest in its natural state, so that when it has to endure heat, chlorine from the pool, braiding and other hair-stressing styling techniques, the strands are stronger and will be able to endure. Even though the elements might damage the hair, the damage won't be as long lasting.

As I've shared with you previously, during my transition to returning my hair to its natural state., I had to endure one of the most difficult times of my life—a divorce. I wasn't even thirty years old, and suddenly I was faced with the decision of whether or not to end my marriage. All the events surrounding that challenge caused me to endure hardship, pain, emotional distress, embarrassment, humiliation, and ridicule. Yet, I was able to endure. I had so many people giving their opinions about what went wrong and what I should do. Some thought I should stay and try to work it out, while others felt I needed to end it. Then, there were people who knew that I was facing a difficult decision, so they had nothing to say at all.

There were times during that process when I didn't think I was going to make it. I mean, I knew I would live and survive, but I wasn't sure how I would make it emotionally. I wasn't quite sure if I'd be able to move forward with my life, reach my goals, and be in a place for love to find me. So many questions constantly went through my mind, but I was prepared for everything. Once I started paying attention and listening to the voice in my heart, I realized that through my hair journey I would gain strength to endure everything that would come my way. And as my hair changed, I changed.

One day, I remember standing in front of the mirror, looking at my hair. I was running my fingers through sections of my wet hair, detangling it with my fingers. There were sections that were coarser than others and were more difficult to detangle. But as I gently finger-combed it, I was able to do it without a lot of my hair breaking off. I remember thinking that God was "detangling" my life. He was sorting things out within me, and I was reminded that I wouldn't break. My hair didn't break because it was stronger now. No chemical or heat damage—just strong, healthy strands of me. So I knew that's why I wouldn't break—because I was strong and healthy, spiritually and emotionally. I knew everything would have an effect on me and I would have to go through some pain. But after the pain subsided, there would still be the promise of God in my life.

We have to go through a lot of challenges in life—broken relationships, problem children, issues with our supervisors and on our jobs—but it is strength that keeps us from losing our minds when we're going through things. When we're confident about who we are, we definitely become stronger. We can look in the mirror and know that we have the strength and power to resist and endure the attacks and forces that come against us. My decision to embrace the journey certainly prepared me for the attacks against my spirit, my character, and my joy.

Being strong doesn't mean that we won't cry or feel sad or experience the range of emotions that accompany life's circumstances. What is means is that we will experience those emotions and go through the tear-filled days and nights, but still have something in our spirits that picks us up when it's time to move forward. Strength is what we have that slowly starts to take the pain away. The Bible speaks about the joy of the Lord being our strength. What that means to me is that when we have joy in our hearts from our relationship with God, we will be able to endure the challenges of life with His strength. We will know that it is all working together for our good and that God has a plan and purpose for our lives.

My hair was a vessel that God used to give me strength to endure the hardships, suffering, and trials that I had to face at that time and in the future.

I Am Bold and Courageous

Isn't it funny that it actually takes courage to be your true self? Sometimes we are required to step outside our comfort zones, be courageous, and actually present our true self to the world. We stand the chance of being judged, ridiculed, condemned, and even misunderstood. Yet, so many times we won't take risks because of fear (I deal with fear in many areas of my life). However, courage is the mental or moral strength to venture, persevere, and withstand danger, fear, or difficulty.

The decision to go natural, for me, took a lot of courage. I was so "comfortable" not standing out and looking like everyone else. I didn't even realize that I didn't look like everyone else anyway. I had other things about me that made me stand out, like my infectious laugh and my warm smile. I didn't even recognize that I already had a "natural energy" that flowed from the inside out, and every new characteristic that would radiate from me as a result of my hair journey had been there all along.

I remember the first time I decided to wear my hair in a natural texture style instead of blown out. The experience was really scary. I had done a two-strand twist-out on my hair and didn't know what to expect. I still had some relaxed hair on the ends, but for the most part it was all natural. I was so nervous. I didn't know what the reaction of the public would be. I didn't know how my family and friends would react to my new look. But I did it anyway. I walked out of my house with bold courage, and from that point forward, I no longer worried about what others thought of me. I was bold enough to look the way I wanted to look and live the way I wanted to live.

I remember having a conversation with a woman who was close to me at the time. She was about fifty-five years old and always wore a relaxed, straight, wrapped hairstyle. People in the room were asking me about my hair and giving their opinions about my new look. I remember her saying that she liked my new look, but she liked my hair straight better and that it "fit" me better. At that moment, I knew that she didn't even really know me. She had known me for a good amount of time, yet she didn't really *know* me. As I thought about her comments, at first I was upset. Then I thought, "Well, she wouldn't know *you* because you haven't shown her *you*." I realized that this journey was also purposed for me to reveal my true self to those in my life, so that they would know exactly who I am.

When a woman decides to step out with a new "do," there has to be a level of courage that accompanies that decision. So many times, we don't have the courage to step out in faith to do the things that we desire to do—not to mention the things that have been *purposed* for us to do. We have to have courage to live outside the prescribed way of thinking and the way people think we should be. It's becoming a trend now for women to "go natural," but the true test to divide those who are following trends from those who have made a commitment to be *free* and *new* will be to examine who has survived when the trend fades, who will survive. Who will still have to courage to remain "natural" when pop culture comes up with something different to focus on?

I Am Capable of Making the Best Decisions for My Life

Through my hair journey I have realized that I do have the ability to discern inner qualities and relationships, and have *insight* to make the right decisions for my life. My decision to go natural went against everything that "made sense" to me. I didn't have the first clue about what to do with my hair. I always kept my hair layered, relaxed, and wrapped. Every now and then I'd venture into some spiral curls or a straw set . . . but I was taking a step into new territory. But somehow, throughout the process, I started learning and understanding more and more about my hair, what it needs to be healthy, andwhich styles look best on me.

Through my day-to-day journey, I have gained understanding and wisdom about my hair and my life. I might be afraid of or not too sure about things going on around me, but when you obtain wisdom, you will have the ability to discern the inner workings of a concept, idea, person, or relationship, and be able to make the best decisions for your life.

As I observed the new texture of my hair as it grew, I started seeing that I had a definitive curl pattern and the texture was manageable. I started watching YouTube tutorials on natural hair styling tips, by some of the noted natural hair contributors and began to experiment with different products. I wore twist-outs, braid-outs, afro puffs, and various other styles that looked good. I eventually learned what was best for my individual hair and didn't really worry too much about what other people were doing. When we're on our journey, we have to learn how to determine what's best for our path. The way to do that is to follow the leading of God as we walk.

John 8:12 says, "Jesus spoke to the people once more and said, 'I am the light of the world. If you follow me, you won't have to walk in darkness, because you will have the light that leads to life.' "

A relationship with God, through Jesus Christ, promises us light. We will not go along our journey in darkness if we are following Him. His love and spirit lights our path and shows us the way to our divine purpose and destiny.

So What Does This Mean for You?

My hair journey is not just about hair. My hair is a lens through which to view my life's journey as I walk in purpose. I was inspired by the words of the song "Strength, Courage, and Wisdom" by India Arie, and the lyrics helped me step out in faith and show my (true) face, because freedom is mine today.

I encourage you to consider the following question as you reflect on your own personal and spiritual journey:

Have you accepted God into your life, and if not, how can you accept Him into your life and heart?

Romans 10:9 says that "If you confess with your mouth that Jesus is Lord and believe in your heart that God raised him from the dead, you will be saved."

You can do it now. You can say the following and you will be saved: "I confess with my mouth and believe in my heart that Jesus is Lord and He died on the cross for my sins and was raised from the dead. I accept Him into my heart now and accept His salvation."

As you move forward through your life, with God leading you, you will begin to see Him and your life in a whole new light. You will begin to experience the joy that comes from knowing Christ and the peace a relationship with Him provides.

Activate the Power

So, here's the big finale! Life is just beginning for you. Every day that you wake up, you are given a new opportunity to start your life over. And no matter what you've been going through in your life, you have the power at your fingertips to change your circumstances. The woman spoken about in the Bible in Luke and Mark, who had been bleeding and hemorrhaging for twelve long years, never gave up. She believed that one day she would be healed from her disease. When she heard about Jesus and how He might be coming through her town, she ran to find Him. But she could only get close enough to touch the hem of His garment, and when she touched it, Jesus felt power leave from Him. He knew that someone had touched Him. When He found out that it was her, He told her that her faith is what healed her. Why in the world would Jesus tell her that? Wasn't *He* the one who was supposed to lay His hands on her and instantly stop the bleeding? Wasn't *He* the one who was supposed to tell the disease to leave her body so that she would be well?

Of course Jesus had the power to do those things. But because this woman had been searching for a cure for twelve years and had gone to every doctor and still didn't give up, and because she found her way to Jesus, whom she knew could heal her, and because she dropped down to the ground and still managed to get to His cloak, and because she *believed*, she was healed. It was her faith that activated the power of God that was then able to heal her. He didn't physically have to touch her body for her to be healed. Just the activation of His power in her heart, spirit, and mind through her faith made her well.

You have the same power! You have the power to activate God in your own life through your faith and belief in Him and His love. We activate his power by reading, meditating on, and believing in His Word. As we read the Word, we become confident in Him and who He is. He speaks to us through Scriptures like Romans 8:18: "Yet what we suffer now is nothing compared to the glory he will reveal to us later" (NLT). And Romans 8:28: "And we know that God causes everything to work together for the good of those who love God and are called according to his purpose for them" (NLT). Also Scriptures like Hebrews 13:5: "Don't love money; be satisfied with what you have. For God has said, I will never fail you. I will never abandon you" (NLT). Or Philippians 1:6: "And I am certain that God, who began the good work within you, will continue his work until it is finally finished on the day when Christ Jesus returns" (NLT) And, one of my personal favorites—Jeremiah 29:11: "For I know the plans I have for you, says the Lord. They are plans for good and not for disaster, to give you a future and a hope" (NLT). These are promises that He's made to us to be with us, take care of us, and never leave us, and these promises give us the hope we need to make it from day to day.

We also activate His power by praying and seeking Him. When we do that, we acknowledge that He is there, ready and willing to answer our call. And even in the midst of our pain, when we worship Him, we activate His presence in our hearts. We recognize that He is God, and He's God even when we don't understand the things going on in our lives.

I tapped into His incredible power as I watched Him transform me through my hair. The hair was His platform to bring my attention directly to Him. As I washed my hair, styled it, monitored its growth, and learned more about how to care for it, He was doing the same with my spirit. He washed me, again, in His precious blood and let me know that I am His. He gave me a new smile, new look, new countenance, and a fresh perspective on who I am. He began to show me the plans for my life and started teaching me how to care for my soul so I'd get to where He wants me to be. He let me know that a little "shedding" every now and then would be normal, because as I walk after His spirit, there would be certain things and people that would fall out of my life. There would be certain desires that would change, and my heart would become more receptive to who He wants me to be.

So, my hope for you is that you will start to look at your own life: the struggles, the pain, the circumstances and events that led you to where you are right now. And see what platform God is using to bring your attention directly to Him. He is standing on the stage of your life, waiting for you to pull back the curtain and invite Him to perform His miracles, wonders, and mighty acts in your life. He's ready and waiting for you to activate His power through a conscious decision to follow Him.

This is my prayer for you:

God, I thank you for being God, my father, my savior, and my friend. I ask that you bless the woman, girl, teenager, or any person who just read this book. I ask, God, that you will use the words to touch her heart and mind and begin a transformation in her life. I pray that she will begin to seek you in a new way, and that because of your grace, mercy, and love, you will activate your power in her life. I ask that you will touch her life and the people around her to see you in a different way and that you will reveal to her the purpose and call for which you've chosen her. I hope that you will allow her to prosper and grow in all endeavors, and that you will place within her a newfound confidence to walk with you. Uplift her spirit and outlook on self. Assure her that she is beautiful because you specifically created her in your image. Thank you for leading her to this book. And for those who do not know you, I pray that they will accept you into their hearts now and begin to live, love, and lead with power.

It is so. Amen.

Excerpts from the Blog
www.spirituallynatural.com:

Sunday, June 6, 2010
a year in the making...

So, this is my first post on my new blog.
On this blog, I will discuss my spiritual journey since deciding to wear my hair natural.

It was one of the best decisions I've ever made and I want to encourage others to do the same.
But, this blog isn't **JUST** about hair.
It's about taking risks, growth, developing new character, and becoming who God always intended us to be....
It's been a year since I've been completely natural and I've learned so much about God, myself, and life since that time.

Feel free to comment, share your stories and experiences with the ways you've experienced your own new growth!!

Tuesday, June 8, 2010
preparation...the "ugly" phase.

I was thinking today about my facebook status post from yesterday...
"In order to change, we have to go through some changes."
This is a very profound statement because sometimes we want change in our lives but we want it to come instantly or in a way that will be comfortable for us.
But, we quickly realize that in order for change to really happen, we have to go through some changes. Some of those changes aren't very happy or comfortable.
They are often difficult and challenging.

So, as I decided to make this physical change from my relaxed hair to my natural hair, I had to go through some changes.
This phase was quickly named, "the ugly phase."
It was ugly because my hair was becoming something that I didn't recognize and I didn't like it.
Mostly because I didn't really know what to do with it.
There were days when I wanted to just go get a relaxer (go back to what was comforting and looked good).
Then, there were other days when I wanted to chop all the relaxer off (something easy to skip the process).

But, I began to understand that it was part of the preparation process.

And, preparation for a greater purpose is sometimes VERY uncomfortable and requires patience.

I had to start paying attention to my hair and spending more time on my hair to come up with styles that looked good.

In this same way, as we prepare to reach our destiny in life, it will require more effort, greater observation to what's going on in and around our lives, and more time spent on actually working to improve our current state.

So, I started researching about what to do with my hair.

At the same time, on this spiritual journey, I began reading my Bible more, talking to God more and asking Him to lead me in all areas of my life.

My hair was growing and so was I...and it was happening quickly.

Normally, your hair grows about 1/2 inch every month.

Mine was growing twice as fast...about 1 inch every month.

At that same rate of growth was my spiritual life.

I was gaining insight to the things of God and I was getting a better understanding of my purpose and who He created me to be.

But, God was also preparing me for the trials that I would face in the months to come.

How can we endure and go through our storms?

By knowing, believing and standing on the very Word and Promises of God.

He was planting His word in my heart so that I would have the strength to endure.

He got my attention through my hair.

As I paid attention to the new growth, I was also paying attention to my new spiritual growth.

This is one of my prayers for those following this blog.

To allow God to prepare you for the destiny He has for you...

Saturday, June 12, 2010
Bold Transition...

Stepping into uncharted or unfamiliar territories can be frightening.

But, most of the time, it's scary because we're concerned about the social consequences for being DIFFERENT.

Thoughts like, "what will people think?" or "people might laugh at me," may cause us not to take the risk of being uniquely different and set apart.

But, when we become bold and realize that there will NEVER come a day when we'll be able to please people, we'll realize that the only thing that matters is doing what God wants us to do.

God sometimes chooses the most unlikely person to fulfill GREATNESS for Him.

Why does He do this?

He does this because He seeks out the heart and not physical appearance.

God chose Mary, a young, poor virgin, to carry His son!

To avoid the consequences of having a single mother situation, He could've easily chosen a 2 parent family, with a kid and a donkey (did they have dogs back then? - LOL).

But, He didn't!

He chose Mary...

Don't you think He knew she'd be ridiculed and that she'd face torment by her village people?

God chose Mary because He knew her heart and the Bible says that He favored her!

He knew she loved Him and that she'd be grateful for the GREATNESS that would be fulfilled through her.

Mary's cousin, Elizabeth even called her blessed because Mary truly believed that what God said to her would be accomplished. (Luke 1:45)

So, as I transitioned into my natural hair, I realized that I'd get some odd stares, some negative comments from some of the people in my life and face some ridicule.

I had women who said to me, "oh, why would you want to do that, you have such beautiful hair," or "I like your hair straight better, it fits you better."

And, the entire time, I'm thinking to myself, so you like the artificial me better...you have accepted this image as who I really am?
You have no clue who I REALLY am...and I am not THIS hair!

But, I didn't worry about PEOPLE and what they thought.
I believed what God said to me would be accomplished.
I believed that through this intimate hair walk, God would do a new thing in me and that old things would pass away and ALL things would become new.
I believed that God would use this journey to bring women closer to Him through this unexplainable, divine connection we have with our hair!
I believed that God would strengthen my spirit as He ministered to me through this hair journey.

I am willing to place the world's view of my "beauty" on the line to fulfill the GREATNESS that God wants to do through me.

It takes boldness and courage but it's worth it...

Tuesday, June 15, 2010
Preparation for the Purpose...God's Timing

It's so amazing how GOD will give us a clear vision, but then the journey or way to the vision seems so cloudy.

I'm learning that this is where God wants us to trust Him.

He knows that sometimes, as flawed humans, we have to be able to "see" something before we will trust Him so He gives us the vision.

The vision is something for us to hold on to as we walk the journey.

The vision is so we will have an end in mind so that we'll keep going.

But, He wants us to trust Him with the path that we are to take to make that vision a reality.

He already knows what mistakes we're going to make, and the "detours" and "distractions" we will create for ourselves along the way.

But, we still have a vision.

And with God's hand upon us, we won't forego the overall vision just because we veered off the path for a moment.

Through a consistent relationship and communication with God, we will maintain our life line to Him.

As I continued on this hair journey, I realized that I was being prepared for my purpose. I now realize that this hair journey is about me becoming a new creature.

There is definitely a spiritual transformation taking place, but it started with something that I never thought I'd do.

The **preparation process** is so important.
The purpose often lies within the process.

For example, if you want a juicy steak on the grilled that's seasoned to perfection, you know that you can't just pull the steak from the freezer and throw it on the grill.

You would follow a specific process: defrost, tenderize, marinate and then grill.

As humans, we don't want to go through the process of being seasoned because often times, it means that we will be beat down, discouraged, get weary and want to give up. We often think about how difficult things are for us and we lose sight of the vision (the promise). The cares of life bog us down to the point where we can't focus on what God has for us.

But, the lessons we will need in order to sustain the vision are learned during the process.

In one of India Arie's songs, she says that "Life is a journey, not a destination."

We're so focused on the destination that we miss the lessons in the journey

I believe that when we focus on the process of preparation, the end result will be more in tune with how God wants it to be.

Tuesday, June 22, 2010
walking towards the light...

As a child, I remember a horror movie called Poltergeist.
And many of you who remember that movie can recall a line or two from it where the little lady was telling Carolanne to "come to the light."
The light was supposed to represent safety from the harm of the evil that was trying to consumer Carolanne.

As I think about my future and destiny, I find that daily, a voice (God, of course) is telling me to "come to the light." The light is the truth about who He is and also who He is within me. My purpose here on earth is the lead others to the light; whether it is by leading them to the right career choice, helping them start a business, teaching them how to set goals and achieve goals or just encouraging someone to look beyond what they see right now. I have a clear purpose for who I am to become in Him because He created that purpose.

So, it's not time for me to become lazy or complacent. As I looked at myself in the morning while rushing to get dressed, I started thinking about how I really need to do my hair. I've been rocking this curly pony puff for about a week and it's such a "lazy" hairstyle for me. Even though it's "cute," it's extremely lazy because it means that I don't have to do anything to it. But, I know that in order for me to get the most of out of my hair, I have to care for it, take time to style it and put the energy and effort into doing so.

I can't become lazy about it because then I'll just settle into this one style and the health of my hair may suffer as a result.

In order for me to be a healthy person in body, mind, spirit, and heart, I must put TIME and ENERGY into developing that woman.

It's imperative...my life depends on it.

So, I have to continue to walk towards the light which is how my journey is illuminated and I'm able to do the things I need to do.

Monday, June 28, 2010
it's the little things...and some hair tips

It's been a while since I've blogged.

This summer is shaping up to be a very interesting one.

I am especially excited about my upcoming 30th birthday (July 24)!!!

Sometimes, when we're in conversation with people, we should really pay attention and hear the revelation behind some of the "little things" that are said.

This week, I was in conversation with several friends and I thought about a few small nuggets of wisdom that stuck with me.

I want to share one of them with you...then at the end of this post, I'm going to post some hair tips for those of you who've been asking me about products and styles.

1. "You are your people." I was with a friend of mine in DC visiting family and as we left, a young lady told my friend "have your people call my people" and my friend responded, "have your people call my people," and the young lady said, "you are your people."

What this says to me is that instead of trying so hard NOT to be like our family or trying so hard to be JUST like our family, we should see our family for who they are and accept what is good for us. Anything that doesn't really line up with who we are as individuals, we should just take it as it is. Much of who we are is attributed to the influences in our lives. Sometimes we allow those influences to shape us TOO much, thus we don't ever really know who we are. We simply become replicates of our mom or dad or uncle or aunt or favorite cousin. However, our family members had their own journeys and they each had to determine the best way for them to go in their lives. Some of our family members would even admit that if they had've had more courage to step out in some areas, they would've made different decisions. True joy in life comes when you're walking in faith trusting God to lead YOU in the direction YOU must go. Your journey is not someone else's. Yes, we are our people, but we are also so much more. We are human. We are spiritual.

We are water. We are light. We are so much more complex as individuals than just a few categories or some socioeconomic status label attached to "our people."

HAIR TIPS:
Several people have asked me what products I use on my hair and what styles I usually wear.
My favorite style right now is the twist out.
I like this style because it's simple and it lasts for a while.
Plus, once it gets "old" it makes a really cute curly fro!

Products I use:
- To cleanse my hair, I use Paul Mitchell Tea Tree shampoo and conditioner or Carol's Daughter Black Vanilla Shampoo/Conditioner and Leave-In conditioner
(I shampoo my hair every other week and I do a "conditioning wash" sometimes twice/week) - A conditioining wash is when you "wash" your hair with only conditioner...not shampoo. Sometimes shampoos will dry out your hair too much.

- For my twists-outs and daily curl definition, I use Miss Jessie's Curly Buttercreme and Baby Buttercreme
Because my hair is naturally curly, after I wash it, I will put the curly buttercreme on it and then use the diffuser on my hair dryer to "set" the curls in.
This makes my curls last a little longer without getting frizzy from the elements outside.

I've also tried Kinky Curly Curling Custard.

I like this product, however, it makes my hair a little hard because it is a natural hair curling "gel" product.

- For moisture I use Raw Shea Butter (melted to an "oil" and rubbed into my scalp and hair)

I am learning how to do more with my hair, so as I learn about new styles and products, I will post!

Monday, August 16, 2010
hard to stay straight...

I got my hair straightened on Friday so that I could get it cut. I wanted to get some of it cut and also since my highlights were growing out, I decided to go ahead and get the rest of the color cut out.

So, it was straight and I went through the entire weekend worrying about keeping it straight. I would flat iron it and the humidity would hit it and it would get puffy.

It was so uncomfortable having to worry about how my hair looked and making sure it kept its style.

I was also worried about continuing to flat iron it because I don't want my hair to stay straight and not be able to go back to its natural texture.

I woke up this morning around 4:45am and couldn't go back to sleep.

So, I decided to get up and twist my hair...When I wet my hair and saw my natural curls I was actually happy.

I felt like myself again. I much rather wear my hair natural than straight.

The message for me in all of this is, I've come to embrace my "new self." Straight hair is a reminder of the old me...always worried about how I look...so self-conscious about appearance and making sure that every hair is in its proper place. So worried that I'll look bad if my hair isn't perfect. I don't live that way anymore. My natural hair is a crown for me. Through this hair journey, I've found confidence and a sense of self that I've never experienced before. I LOVE the way I feel about myself and it shows.

So, I rather be true to who I've become and who I am than to try to go back and forth with something that's really not me.

I know it's good to be versatile and flexible, but straight hair (for me) is so overrated right now. It's conventional, regular, and hard for me to maintain.

And maybe I'll revisit the straight look later, but for now, I think I'll keep flowing naturally!!!

The message for you...Be YOU! Once you realize who you are, be that! Don't allow pressures to look like others or be like others cause you to veer from who you know you really are! Dare to be unique and to be the individual that you were created to be. Others will be blessed as a result of you being true to who you are.

Sunday, November 21, 2010
what now?!

In life, we sometimes get to a point where we're tired of the routine, day to day, system of life. We get "stuck," so to speak, in a mundane, monotonous way of living and we need a little boost. Sometimes, the boost happens by way of a vacation or a shake up in our routine. Sometimes, we just remain stuck!

Well, I'm at a point where I feel "stuck" with my hair...Don't get me wrong, I'm still LOVING and embracing my natural. However, I am getting to a point where I want to do something different with my hair. I want to be able to try new styles, experiment with different products and just take it to another level.

In other words, I want GROWTH.
Not just an actual growth of my hair, but a growth of my outlook about this journey. I want my sense of who I am with this hair to grow and I want to see some changes in my life as a result of this journey.

As I was perusing the site of **www.Curlynikki.com** (a very good natural hair resource site), I thought about how much effort and energy Nikki puts into updating her website and giving out information about products and styles. Even her subscribers spend time giving information about their hair. But in order to do that, they have to actually DO the things they are recommending. So, they have committed themselves to their natural journey. As with any commitment in life, sometimes it calls for us to renew that sense of commitment so that we can keep moving forward and stay motivated for the journey.

So, I'm renewing my commitment to this journey and I'm going to put more effort into getting the growth I want for my hair (and my life)! Change is on the way.

Monday, November 22, 2010
subtle change is STILL change!

So, I was feeling the way I was feeling yesterday and today I decided to do something about it!!!
I'm in "doing" mode now...
So, I decided to buy some Henna powder to give my hair a subtle color change and extra "boost."
Henna is an organic way to color your hair and it is a natural conditioner that adds shine. I've never used it before but I've heard great things about it!
Nevertheless, I wanted a change, but I'm also realistic about who I am and I knew I wouldn't be ready for a DRASTIC change to my hair.
So, I'm going to try something new, but subtle.

We should definitely not hesitate to make decisions about changes that we want to see in our lives, but we should also remain realistic about how much we are equipped to handle at that time. It's important not to move too quickly into decisions because we could end up regretting the very thing that we thought we wanted.

So, I'll keep you all posted on how the Henna color treatment goes...and I'll post pics.

Thursday, January 13, 2011
Growth! That's my GOAL!

The start of a new year always causes people to make these "resolutions" where they resolve to do something differently than previous years or to quit a specific behavior or action. I believe people make resolutions because they feel that the start of a new year means that something has to change.
They believe that their life should look differently than the year before or else they really haven't taken full advantage of a new year.

A resolution is the formal expression of an opinion or intention or a determination.
The tone of a resolution is that there is some problem that needs to be solved.
Sometimes, it's difficult for me to view my behaviors or actions as "problems" that need to be solved.
I just like to identify my target goal and align my thoughts and actions to achieve that goal.

Therefore, for 2011, as I've done in previous years, I have set A goal...and it's a simple ONE...**GROWTH**!

My goal is to experience GROWTH in every area of my life:

- Spiritual
- Financial
- Family
- Relationship/Social
- Health/Physical
- Educational
- Career

How in the world will I achieve growth in each of these areas?

Well, just like the process of growing hair (which grows about 1/2 to 3/4 inch every month), I will have to place attention, care, and effort into the areas I desire to see growth.

When I want my hair to grow, I must keep my scalp clean, comb/brush my hair, obtain regular trims and place care into styling.

In the same manner, I must give attention to my financial life by using more wisdom with how to spend my money, creating a budget for spending and saving, seeking ways to earn additional income to reach my savings goals, pay down debts, and seek out better ways to manage my money.

For relational and social growth, I must cultivate current relationships and establish deeper connections with my family and friends. And, I will put myself in more diverse social environments that will enhance my network and ability to relate to other people.

I could go on with other examples, but I will allow you to think about how to reach growth in various areas of your life.

So, I'll check in often with lessons and reports on my GROWTH this year!

Til next time...

Tuesday, February 15, 2011
these are my confessions...

So, I have a CONFESSION!!

I am AFRAID!
WOW...that was more difficult than I thought it would be!
I am admitting to everyone (ok, whoever will read this), that I deal with fear!

Why in the world would I be afraid?

I didn't really know how to describe my fear until TODAY after a conversation with a friend and mentor who guided me to this conclusion:

I'm afraid of myself!

I know that doesn't make much sense, but this is what I'm saying...

I'm afraid of the power that is within me!

I'm afraid of the consequences AND responsibilities that come with who I am and who God made me.

I'm afraid of doing the things that I am purposed to do because of what will happen as a result (in my life and the lives of others)...change, growth, empowerment, increased knowledge, new life, joy, wealth, etc.

I'm afraid of myself!

As soon as I started writing this post, I thought about the famous quote by Franklin Roosevelt where he said the "only thing to fear is fear itself" but what in the world does that mean to me?

It means that when I fear I LOSE my power.

So, I should actually fear being afraid because it leaves me powerless.

It keeps me from moving into my purpose and destiny and keeps me in a place of uncertainty, doubt, lack, and despair.

Well, TODAY, I am making the decision to acknowledge the fear and walk away from it.

- I am determined to have the power, love and sound mind that Paul spoke about in the Bible.

- I am determined to stop negative thoughts that keep me from being able to will God's blessings into my life.

Life is a challenging journey...but one assurance that we all have is that it will end.

I don't want to live a life of fear and doubt. I want to leave my mark on this world by living out my purpose and knowing that who I was made a difference to someone.

I will continue this discussion as I fight, pray, and live through it.

If you deal with fear (of anything) and it's holding you back (I'm pretty sure it is) in any way, then I'd challenge you to acknowledge it, name it, then make a decision to either continue to let it follow/lead you or to walk away from it! NO MORE FEAR!

Saturday, February 26, 2011
Growth requires honesty and commitment

Yesterday, as I talked to my friend Crystal about the current state of her hair, I realized a few things through her hair journey.

Crystal has been natural for over 10 years. So she came into the game before it was a "trend" or movement. Since her first big chop she has worn Afros, twist outs, braids, head wraps, had other big chops and other styles. For much of the past 10 yrs her relationship and treatment of her hair resembled the flow and movement of her life's experiences. One day, I'm sure you will read about some of those in a book OR maybe even a guest post on my blog. (Wink wink).

However, a few yrs ago she moved back home to care for her mother who was in kidney failure (last October she was blessed with a kidney transplant). Well, the verdict is still out on the reason why she experienced it but Crystal found herself in a situation where she was losing hair. Her hair was breaking off and shedding in an unhealthy way. She knew she needed to focus on it and get it to grow again but she was honest with herself. She knew that the combo of everything going on in her life and her lack of desire to actually commit to the work of cultivating her hair was not a good one. So she made the decision to get her first sew-in. She was committed to growth but she was honest with herself about her comfort level of involvement in the process.

Since making that decision last year, she has been wearing sew-ins and making sure her hair and scalp stays clean, moisturized and conditioned. Recently, she got a "fresh" sew-in and she reported to me that her hair has grown and is much healthier. SN: I was a lil perturbed because she didn't let me see it... But she said that she's happy about the progress she's made with her hair.

I think her process resembles the process of many of us who want growth. We sometimes see the damage or breakage in certain areas of our lives and we know something must be done. But, we are not honest with ourselves about the level of commitment or involvement we are comfortable with. If we were more honest with ourselves and came up with alternate ideas about how to achieve our desired outcome, we would probably succeed.

I believe Crystal experienced some personal growth from this process as well because she made a point to tell me that in years prior she had not been upfront with herself about her willingness to work with her hair. She would do different things to it and sometimes would just cut it off and start over. But, this time she did something different. She had a goal in mind and she knew what she would and wouldn't do; so she aligned her actions and choices with that. I believe that her expectancy was different this time as well because she knew she was doing something she had never done before.

I have learned a lot from her story of growth and as I continue on my journey I'll be mindful that growth requires honesty and com

Wednesday, March 23, 2011
Recognize I'm Back!

Ok, so I was thinking the other day about how my life has completely changed over the past couple of years.
But, most of the changes, even those that were tumultuous, were for my good and have worked out to be for the best!

I recognize, now, that who I became for about 7 years was not who I was at all.

I was walking around with straight, flat hair, an affect just as flat, wearing no make up, not communicating and relating to my friends on a regular basis, and without LIFE!

Sure, I was alive, but I wasn't LIVING!

I was simply existing and surviving in my chosen environment.

Now, as I enter in another Spring season of LIFE, I'm so grateful to be BACK to myself.

Through my hair journey, I've rediscovered who I am and what is important to me.

I believe that this energy that's so inspired by my hair gives me the confidence to be myself and know that who I am is actually ok.

I don't have to dumb down, water down and play down who I am.

As women, or even people, we should have the freedom to walk out our purposed life journey with only a concern for who God wants us to be.

To be able to live life to the fullest, without regard to what others say about me is a great feeling.

It's nice to be free from the judgment of others and be able to live for God the way HE wants me to live.

I'm on a journey.

I'm walking towards the vision that God has given me for my life...

And, I feel glad about it!

Can I get an Amen!?

LOL

Sunday, March 27, 2011
We could all use an Adjustment Bureau...

Last night, I went to see the movie, *The Adjustment Bureau*. I thought it was an excellent movie and more than that, it was thought-provoking and incited me to really examine myself. As I watched the movie, I realized a lot about myself and my view of life and purpose.

I don't want to get into the plot of the movie, but I wanted to share something that stood out to me and how I plan to apply it to my life.

LOVE IS OUR PURPOSE.

I am a strong believer in God. And I truly understand the power of Love and how when God is in our lives, we will know how to love.

However, sometimes, I tend to be so "purpose-driven," that I neglect the importance of LOVE in my life. Receiving love from others and also showing love to others.

I believe that I know how to love, but at the point where it "interferes" with my purpose, I don't always focus on it. However, LOVE is the foundation of our purpose in life.

Then, I thought about 1 Corinthians 13, which is the scripture where Paul talks about Love. Sometimes, I focus on the part that says what Love is, but I was forced to think about the first part of that passage which is,

"1 If I speak in the tongues[a] of men or of angels, but do not have love, I am only a resounding gong or a clanging cymbal. 2 If I have the gift of prophecy and can fathom all mysteries and all knowledge, and if I have a faith that can move mountains, but do not have love, I am nothing. 3 If I give all I possess to the poor and give over my body to hardship that I may boast,[b] but do not have love, I gain nothing."

So, as I think about it, Paul was saying that nothing we do in life matters if we don't have love. I may have gifts and be able to do great THINGS for God, but if I don't have love, then it doesn't matter.

The movie reinforces this thought. Love is the central theme even though when you watch it you might think that the central theme is purpose. But, that's just it...LOVE IS OUR PURPOSE! And we should make every effort to walk and live in love...in love with God and with each other.

If you've seen it, let me know what you think and what you took away from it!

Sunday, May 1, 2011
An Acceptable Sacrifice

So, it's the first day of May! WOW!
I'm so excited about the Spring season.
I definitely went through a WINTER season of my life this year and I'm ready for the newness that Spring brings.
There are opportunities on the horizon and plenty of blessings on the way from above!
It's so exciting to think about the beautiful sunshine, flowers, and warm breezes throughout the entire day!
Not to mention, the chirping of the birds and sights and sounds of children playing outside after school.

For me, the Spring season brings an opportunity to RENEW my commitment to spiritual growth.
Two years ago this month, I cut out the last of my relaxer and started this New Growth hair journey!
I was in transition prior to that, but the day I cut out the last 3 inches of my relaxed hair was the beginning of a NEW me.
I continue my hair journey, but now it's time for another type of transformation...but, still New Growth.

NOW, I'm commiting myself to a healthier lifestyle.
I'm ready for change in my mind, **BODY**, and spirit.

This process begins with a mental and spiritual commitment to living a healthier lifestyle by gaining discipline and making healthier choices with nutrition and exercise.

What does this mean for ME?
I've made the DECISION to live healthier.
And just like any other DECISION in our lives, there will be pros and cons.
But, it means that I'm going to choose healthier foods to eat, and commit to a more active lifestyle through exercise.
By eating more nutrient dense fruits and vegetables and choosing lean proteins and low and no fat dairy products, limiting sugar and fat intake and exercising regularly, I will transform!
I'm not going to put pressure on myself to "lose weight" because if I focus on my health, weight loss will be the end result, in addition to healthier hair, clearer skin, and numerous other health benefits.
When we focus on the right thing, benefits are inevitable.

It's like the scripture Matthew 6:33 that says "But seek first his kingdom and his righteousness, and all these things will be given to you as well" (NIV). When we seek to please God and live according to His definition of what is righteous and what is good, then everything that is supposed to happen in our lives will. He will take care of us when we focus on Him!

My spiritual journey will now include this new commitment.

I present my body as a living sacrifice....

Romans 12 (New Living Translation)

A Living Sacrifice to God

[1] And so, dear brothers and sisters, I plead with you to give your bodies to God because of all he has done for you. Let them be a living and holy sacrifice—the kind he will find acceptable. This is truly the way to worship him. [2] Don't copy the behavior and customs of this world, but let God transform you into a new person by changing the way you think. Then you will learn to know God's will for you, which is good and pleasing and perfect.

Thursday, June 9, 2011
Not just another "me, too"

Recently, I met with 2 retired executives with SCORE (Service Corps of Retired Executives) to receive some free business counseling for my consulting firm. As they gave their recommendations one of them talked about finding your niche. As he talked about setting yourself apart and figuring out what you do better than anyone else, he quickly stated, "don't just be a me too."

I actually stopped to think about what he was saying and once I realized what he said I immediately grabbed on to the application of that statement in my life.

We all have gifts, talents and abilities. But we have to use those unique gifts in ways where we stand out and apart from everyone else. As a special creature made by God, we each have a distinct place in the Earth. So it's up to us to find that place. Plenty of people can sing. But what sets the talent of someone like Jennifer Hudson apart from another gifted singer. A lot of times it is drive and the willingness to step out and pursue a dream or goal.

I don't want to just be a "me, too" who goes through life doing what everyone else does. I want to be set apart and special.

Even when it comes to my personal style and image I want to stand out for my uniqueness and confident approach to my physical appearance. Don't just be a "me, too."

Time to #standout #justsaying

Thursday, August 11, 2011
Greatness Is Not By Chance

During the past year, I've experienced a major "shifting" in my life.
I use the word "shifting" as opposed to "shift" because it is actively taking place, even as I type.
You might not understand what I'm talking about so let me help you understand.

Over the past two years I've experienced the following (not necessarily in this order, but pretty close)...

- *Sold a house; moved into an apartment*
- *Got divorced*
- *Was laid off from a job*
- *Started developing a small business*
- *Started my natural hair journey*
- *Started this blog*
- *Turned 30*
- *Wrote a book about that hair journey*
- *Used public assistance (unemployment) to support myself*
- *Developed new friendships/relationships that will be lifelong*
- *Strengthened old relationships*
- *Applied for countless jobs*
- *Interviewed for some great positions*
- *Applied for and accepted to a PhD program*
- *Hired for a management position at a major globally acclaimed institution*

These are just a few of the life changes I've recently experienced. Not to mention that my personal life has taken quite a few interesting turns of its own.

So, I choose to say, instead of saying I've experienced problems or challenges, that my life is shifting.

During a shift, there are some things that happen in our lives that cause us to STOP in our idea of movement and take a look at what is happening in our lives and around our lives.

If you remember, as a child, standing on a carousel that is moving, you remember that if you moved too much during the movement of the carousel you would get dizzy and often stumble and sometimes even fall down.
So, normally, you would stand still and hold on to one of the poles that supported the carousel animals.

The purpose of the shift in life is to prepare us to walk in our purpose and destiny.
I am a believer that greatness is not an accident and doesn't **JUST** happen.
There is purpose in everything that happens in our lives that leads us to a place of purpose and destiny.
In other words, stop trying to figure out why you're going through life's shift and just hold on.
Many times, we feel that we must "keep it moving."
Our culture makes those of us who are ambitious, goal-oriented and purpose-driven feel that we need to constantly move so that we won't be left out or left behind.

But sometimes movement actually means standing still and allowing movement to take place around us and shift our current position in life. It doesn't mean that we aren't always thinking, conceptualizing and dreaming, but it just means that we take the time to stop and see where we are and use that view to help us figure out the next move.

Just like that carousel that is moving even while we are standing still; life is similar.

Sometimes life is moving all around us and as we stand still we are able to see different perspectives as it moves.

The position in life where we are walking in purpose and living our dreams, sometimes requires that our perspective change.

We don't always **SEE** things the way we need to see, so when we are able to stop and watch the movement around us, our eyes are opened in a new way.

We are able to define who we are and what it is we are here on Earth to do.

Each of us has a divine purpose, which is great in one way or another, but often, life's circumstances and situations cause us to lose sight of that purpose and we end up moving our feet but not walking in or on purpose.

You are on the brink of greatness and there is something that you must **SEE** before you can take the actions that will eventually lead you to greatness.

So, stand still, hold on, keep dreaming, see what you need to see, then **ACT** accordingly.

Your destiny is not going to be by chance...
It's on purpose...be still, so you can walk into it!

Thursday, September 22, 2011
Stretch...you'll feel better!

I was sitting at my desk and was feeling really drained.

In August, I started a new job and a PhD program and I've been going full speed ever since.

I feel like I haven't had much time to enjoy the leisurely activities that I did during my time of unemployment (rest).

And, oh how I miss my Zumba classes (I need to find some that fit into my schedule ASAP)!

But, as I sat and thought about how tired I felt, I decided to stand up and stretch.

I walked over to the window in my office, lifted my arms above my head and pulled my body into a deep stretch...then, I bent down and stretched my back and legs. When I stood up, I felt much better!

I felt a lot of the tightness and tension leave my body and even felt a burst of energy that helped me continue the rest of the day.

I think life sometimes requires us to stretch to feel better.

We often become bogged down with the routine and tired from all of the roles we play in life.

When we're able to "stretch" our minds and our spirits to focus on something else, it often helps us feel a lot better.

But, how do we "stretch," mentally, spiritually and emotionally?

Do something different to change your perspective about where you are and what's important
- Take a leisurely walk with no clear destination - observe, meditate, smile
- Eat your lunch outside
- Start a conversation with a stranger
- Take a moment to stand outside and look up in the sky (it's amazing how much clarity you receive when you realize how small you are in this giant world)
- Take deep breaths (you will notice how very little we are actually breathing!)

These may seem like really simple acts, but how often do you really take a minute to do such things?
How often do we feel like we don't have the time to take a minute and enjoy life and our surroundings?
What are some of the things you do to "stretch" throughout the day?

Tuesday, October 25, 2011
If He brought you to it...

For anyone who has ever actively attended church, or Sunday school, you've heard different "cliche-like" terms that have become commonplace in the church.

For example,

"I'm too blessed to be stressed, too anointed to be disappointed," or

"If it had not been for the Lord who was on my side, where would I be?"
or my personal favorite,

"God is good, all the time and ......c'mon you know what to say....all the time, God is good." RIGHT!!! :-)

And, while most of these terms are based on scripture or someones personal testimony, they often are repeated in concert by the church with no real connection to the message behind the cliche. In some cases, they have become ways for people to sound and be, what I like to call, "**churchy.**"

As you develop a personal relationship with God, our creator, you start to get a better understanding of what people really mean and feel when they say things like that.
YOU start to understand and even witness the actual goodness of God in your own life and even through the difficult times, you learn that God IS good!

Well, I was thinking about where I am right now and what I should blog and one of these "churchy cliches" came to mind and it is reflective of where I have been and where I am and probably where I'll continue to be.

"If He brought you to it, He'll take you through it!"

This message popped into my mind and I started to think about all the things He (God) had brought me TO. For the purposes of my relationship with God, I look at "brought me" the same as "allowed." I believe that God, in many situations, ALLOWS us to endure different situations and doesn't necessarily bring those situations upon us.

Nevetheless...

He "brought me" to a period of unemployment and "lack," but eventually, I walked with Him through it and now I'm gainfully employed.

He "brought me" to a period of loneliness and heartache, but as I continued to keep my eyes on Him, I'm experiencing more joy in my life because I'm surrounded by love from family and friends.

And those are just two examples of how I've witnessed this saying in my own life.

Usually, people use this saying to encourage others during times of hardship and suffering.

We are encouraging them to keep their focus on God and He will bring us through every situation because He will never leave us or forsake us.

But, recently, I've had to shift the relevance and application of this saying to my life right now.

Now, I'm at a place where God is actually bringing me to some of His PROMISES for me!

YAY!!

So many incredible opportunities to live out my dreams and to fulfill His destiny for me, are right at my fingertips, and I'm excited, but somewhat fearful of what lies ahead.

So, when I think about the phrase, "If He brought you to it, He'll take you through it," I think it also applies to the good times and His promises.

Often, we are more fearful of the promises than we are of the pain.

Our pain becomes so much of a consistent part of life that we can't imagine a life without pain and heartache or disappointment.

So, when we begin experiencing the harvest season of life, we can't even believe that God really does allow His Son and sun to shine in our lives.

So we become afraid instead of believing that if He promised it and brought it to us, then we will get to the other side of that promise into destiny!

The good news is that, if we are in relationship with Him, God will walk in front of us allowing his favor to go before us into places that we would never imagine and He's walking beside us to help us learn how to experience Him through faith.

If He brought you to it (*allowed it to happen in your life, sent his abundant blessings your way, answered your prayers, making all things work together for your good*), then He will bring you through it (*to a place of destiny, fruitfulness, and joy*).

Monday, November 7, 2011
This "patient love"

One of my favorite definitions of love is located in the book of 1 Corinthians. In the 13th chapter, Paul writes about the importance of love and gives his understanding of what love is and is not. He leads into the definition by saying that if we have all of these talents and abilities but do not have love then nothing else really matters. In verse 4, he begins to really get into the description of love:

"Love is patient, love is kind. It does not envy, it does not boast, it is not proud. It does not dishonor others, it is not self-seeking, it is not easily angered, it keeps no record of wrongs. Love does not delight in evil but rejoices with the truth. It always protects, always trusts, always hopes, always perseveres." (1 Corinthians 13:4-7)

The very first adjective that Paul uses to describe love is the word PATIENT. What does he really mean by using this term to describe love? Many people view the word love as a noun. They look at it as something that we possess or hold in our hearts. Others view the word love as a verb, because it is seen as something that we do; an action. Whichever way you look at it, Paul says that it's "patient."

If we look at the word, patient, and it's definition we find:

1. capable of waiting: able to endure waiting, delay, or provocation without becoming annoyed or upset

2. capable of persevering: able to persevere calmly, especially when faced with difficulties

So, does this mean that love waits and endures without becoming annoyed or upset? Does it mean that it perseveres through difficulty in a calm manner? For Paul, apparently so.

But, how can we love patiently or experience a patient love when everything in our society and culture speaks contrary to this idea? Usually, when we say that we love someone or believe that someone loves us, we automatically start the clock. We begin to put time frames on our lives and theirs simply because love is present. In relationships, people automatically start planning the engagement or the wedding once someone used the term love.

I'd like to think, however, that love is just the beginning of building a solid foundation for a relationship. It takes time to create the type of love that Paul describes in 1 Corinthians 13, which is why I think he started with "love is patient." The word love should not be pressure filled and create stress and anxiety for those who give or receive it. God's desire is for everyone to love and be loved. This "patient love" is what many people, especially those who desire to be married, need to learn and practice. Before thinking about the wedding or your ideal honeymoon destination, perhaps couples should learn to love patiently. Love in a way where they are waiting for the right timing to move into the next step. Loving patiently might mean taking time to learn about someone's values, goals, dreams, and spiritual desires. Loving patiently might mean being in a relationship but also vigorously pursuing your own destiny, dreams and God-given purpose as he or she does the same so that should the relationship grow into more, the two will be whole and complete before joining as one.

Perhaps if we learn how to love patiently, we will learn more about God and how to love Him and do more of what He desires of us. An evaluation of past mistakes helped me understand how I need to live and enforce a patient love. I'm happy because I see the results of being patient and not having so many pressure filled expectations of those we love. God desires to teach us how to give and receive love His way.

Just remember that all things work together for our good if we LOVE Him and are called according to His purpose (Romans 8:28). So, as long as we keep loving God and living out His purpose for our lives, everything else will come together for our good. So, practice more patience in your love for others. If you are married, be more patient with your spouse. If you are a parent, be more patient with your children. In your relationships, practice waiting without becoming annoyed and trust God to work it out for your good. Focus on becoming a better person, pursue your dreams and walk in your destiny.

In the words (and voice) of Pastor Joel Osteen, "Do you believe it on today?" :-)

About the Author

Margaret A. Brunson was born and raised in North Carolina. She was born to Dr. Jesse and Mrs. Doris Brunson, who were and continue to be very devoted godly parents who nurtured her and raised her to be a free servant of God. They taught her principles of God and encouraged her to set her goals and aim high. She grew up with her older brother, Jesse Wayne, and they experienced life as "preacher's kids." She now has a beautiful sister-in-law, Marvella, a vibrant, full-of-life niece, Zari (whom she greatly adores), and a handsome fun-loving little nephew, Elias!

Margaret places much value on education and its power to increase knowledge and create change in lives. She graduated high school in Fayetteville, NC, and attended the University of North Carolina at Chapel Hill, where she obtained a bachelor of arts degree in psychology in 2002. Later, she attended North Carolina Central University in Durham, NC, and earned a master's of public administration in 2009. She is currently a doctoral student at North Carolina A&T State University in Greensboro, NC, pursuing a PhD in leadership studies.

Margaret is active in her local community and is a member of the Eta Phi Zeta Chapter of Zeta Phi Beta Sorority, Inc. Her passion involves allowing the love and power of a relationship with God to encourage and motivate people to find purpose, follow their dreams, and reach their full potential in life. She longs for a day when young people will overcome low self-esteem, discover their divine purpose, and be who God wants them to be. Since she was married and divorced by the age of thirty, Margaret is now dedicated to helping young women realize who they are so they will learn to make the best choices for their lives.

Because of her decisions, mistakes, and pain, she is able to encourage and inspire based on her own *real life* experiences. If you would like to contact Margaret A. Brunson, check out her website and blog: www.spirituallynatural.com, "Like" *New Growth: How My Hair Saved My Life* on Facebook, or follow her on Twitter @MBisFree.

CPSIA information can be obtained at www.ICGtesting.com
Printed in the USA
BVOW081104020413

317077BV00001B/73/P